". . . you must not repeat what I'm about to say . . . we may have an outbreak of the plague here in the village that could wipe us all out and . . . a massive hurricane is headed our way, hell, right for us, and we have a serial killer running around the island somewhere. How's that for a Tuesday afternoon in September?"

CAPE HATTERAS MYSTERIES

SOUND & FURY

FRED HALE

SANDY BAY PUBLISHING
HATTERAS, NC 27943

This book is a work of fiction set in a background of Cape Hatteras, North Carolina. A few natives and locals appear in the story under their right names. Their portraits are offered as essentially truthful, though scenes and dialogue involving both real and fictitious characters are invented. Any other usage of real people's names is coincidental. Any resemblance of the imaginary characters to actual persons living or dead is unintended.

SOUND & FURY
February, 1998

Book and Cover Design by Jo Anne W. Hale

ISBN: 1-57502-822-0

Printed in the United States of America by

MORRIS PUBLISHING
3212 East Highway 30 • Kearney, NE 68847 • 1-800-650-7888

ACKNOWLEDGMENTS

Once again my many thanks to all of those who have helped me with the Cape Hatteras Mysteries series. A special thanks to Elaine, Jo Anne, Anne, Dee, Ken and Dr. Al Hodges. Any medical misadventures are entirely mine.

FGH

For Glenn Adele Evelyn
a gracious and loving lady,
my Mother

*"Life's but a walking shadow, a poor
     player
That struts and frets his hour upon the
     stage,
And then is heard no more; it is a tale
Told by an idiot, full of sound and
     fury,
Signifying nothing."*

William Shakespeare

SOUND & FURY

Chapter 1

The speed limit in Hatteras Village is 25 miles per hour and I was doing at least 45 as I raced across the bridge at the slash, braked and skidded through a high speed left turn into the parking lot for the Medical Center. Riding shotgun for me, with his front paws braced against the windshield, was my faithful companion, Amos, a very large Golden Retriever. In the back of the truck were a father and son, one near death. I pulled up near the emergency door and killed the engine on my 'nother truck.

Until recently I owned a red Ford Ranger, but now I have a 'nother truck, a used (previously owned) maroon 4x4 Ford F-150; full sized and vigorous. Because of the wind and salt and occasional flooding, no sane native or local resident of the North Carolina Outer Banks ever buys a new truck. New trucks are for tourists. We buy 'nother trucks, as in "Is that a new truck, Fred?" And I answer, "Nah. Just a 'nother truck." Shiny new trucks with all working doors and windows are not for us "Bankers."

By the time I had jumped out and run to the tailgate, a wet and muddy Ed Gilliam had climbed off the truck and had his bloody, muddy son in his arms. This had not been an easy task, for "little" Eddie is about thirty, stands six feet four and is much larger than "Big" Ed who is six feet and maybe two hundred. Now, I'm no shrinking violet, about 240, and I tried to maneuver into position to help at the steps leading up to the side door, but finally just got out of the way and let Ed handle it. At the top I held the door open as Ed pushed by me and turned left into the emergency examining room. I headed down the hall looking for help and ran right into Doctor Tom Allen.

"What the hell's going on, Fred?" He looked at me questioningly. "Whom did you bring in?"

"Eddie Gilliam. He sank in the mud. We were working on a bulkhead and he stepped into a hole and disappeared . . . but we got him out!"

We entered the emergency room together. "He

drowned? You got him breathing?" Doc asked anxiously.

"He's breathing, but unconscious," I said. "He went into the mud under the water. Kind of like quicksand. When we pulled him out, he'd stopped breathing and his mouth was full of mud. Cleaned that out but mud was in his throat. Completely clogged. Couldn't breathe. I tried to clear the mud with my finger but couldn't, so I used my pocket knife and did a tracheotomy. That's where the blood is from."

Ed was holding his son upright in the examining chair with mud and water dripping onto the spotless tile floor. Doc Tom quickly checked for breathing and then lowered the chair back, turning it into an examining table. He turned Eddie onto his stomach and pulled his head to one side.

"Nice cut, Fred. Where'd you learn to do that? Forget it, I don't have time for one of your meandering stories. Get the hell out of here and let the nurses help me. How long was he under?"

"Maybe three or four minutes," I said.

"Okay, get!" He shouted.

For a Monday morning in September, the waiting room was unusually slow – just three patients waiting, none of whom I recognized. They all looked up as Ed and I entered through the swinging

doors from the hall, quickly followed by Kim
Smith, a lab assistant.

"Would you like to clean up in the restroom,
Mister Gilliam?" She asked as Deputy Sheriff
Brian Lynch pushed the front door open and ambled
in, his bulk essentially filling the end of the room.

I know most all the deputies because I'm a
Special Deputy for Dare County under Sheriff
Thomas "Matt" Mathews who is an old friend and
poker playing buddy. I'm not a full time paid
deputy or anything like that, but Matt calls upon me
from time to time to help out with interesting or
difficult cases. I'm an engineer, mostly retired, do
some writing, still have some business ventures that
include repairing bulkheads, and I hire out as an
energy consultant from time to time if the job
appears interesting. Over the past few years I've
helped Matt solve a couple of murders, and I've
become a sounding board for him. On occasion, I've
also been helpful in cutting through red tape and
bureaucratic bullshit through some powerful friends
I left behind in Washington, D.C., when Jo Anne
and I moved to the Outer Banks some ten years
ago.

"What brings you here, Brian?" I asked.

"Dog bite." He said through gapped front teeth.
"You?"

"Nope. I got called by Doctor Allen. Some tourist got bit while on the beach. Checked the dog out and he had all his shots. Why you here, Fred?"

"Little Eddie Gilliam darned near drowned this morning while we, him and me and Ed senior, were working on a bulkhead job in Hatteras Estates. The Funke property on the canal. You know where it is?"

"No. Not exactly, but isn't all that water shallow? I mean, not more than three or four feet deep at the most? Can't even get a big boat in there."

"Yeah, but he stepped into a hole we had blown out and sank. He was working in the water with waders on and Ed senior and I were working the bank side. We were refacing the bulkhead where some of the boards were losing sand through worm holes and causing erosion, but instead of taking everything apart we were just washing out about three feet of mud at the bottom and slapping new boards over top of the old ones. We had our pump sitting on the bank taking a suction from the sound and using our big fire hose . . ."

"Yeah."

"It puts out a hell of a lot of pressure and a lotta water. Anyway, Eddie was in the water with the hose and had just washed out another hole for the next board when he stepped toward the bank and sunk. We'd been having trouble with the holes. We'd blow mud out and slide a 2x10 vertically in place and sometimes it would sink before Eddie could get a nail in it. It was almost like once you moved some of the mud there wasn't any bottom. We warned him to be careful . . . in fact I wanted him to put on a safety line but he said he didn't need it. Well, he stepped into a hole and his waders filled with water and he sank into the mud out of sight."

"Sunk out of sight?" Sergeant Lynch shook his head in amazement. "How'd you get him out?"

"You aren't going to believe it. We had a nylon rope, about fifty feet long, with us and Ed tied it around his waist and told me to tie the end to my truck which was parked near by and he jumped in the water. The end of the hose was loose in the canal, jumping around like a damn snake, and Ed got hold of it and yelled for me to count to twenty and start pulling him out. Then, he moved to where Eddie went under and turned the hose down and started blowing out a huge hole. Then . . . he stepped into it and disappeared under the water and into the mud. Scared the hell out of me. I thought he was crazy . . . thought I'd lost him, too. I still had the line in my hand and I tied it to the front bumper and got in the truck, shifted to four wheel drive and started backing up. I was worried that the rope would break. I really was. My heart was beating a mile a minute. I forgot all about counting to twenty . . ."

My mind flashed back to the truck. "I was worried that the rope would break . . . cut by the bumper or snagged on the bulkhead . . . my heart was pounding in my ears . . . I was gunning the truck's engine and I was backing . . . and suddenly I heard Ed yell, 'Keep pulling! Keep pulling, I think I got him hooked with my foot! Pull faster. I'm losing it. Dammit! Faster. I got him! I got him! Stop. Fuckin' stop the truck. NOW!! YOU SONOFABITCH, STOP . . . NOW!!'"

I looked around the waiting room. There was shocked silence. All eyes were on me.

Sergeant Lynch just kept shaking his head and he said, "You were shouting. Calm down, man."

I was sweating and breathing fast. I looked at him and as he slowly came into clear focus, I felt my body surrender to my emotions. I was hollow inside and I became aware that I had a dull headache.

I started to sit down and stopped. I was dirty and wet.

"So, what happened?" Lynch asked.

I knew that in less than an hour this story would sweep from one end of the island to the other, so I had to make certain that I got it right.

I looked at the ceiling and back to the floor. My tone was serious and low. "Well, where was I?" I asked the hushed room. "Oh, yes, I was in the truck and backin' and I heard shouting and I stopped and set the brake and hurried back to the canal bank. Ed was holding onto the bulkhead with one hand and had his other arm through the shoulder straps of his son's waders. He said he still didn't have a bottom and for me to grab Eddie. I did and Ed pulled himself up over the bulkhead and helped me pull little Eddie out of the water . . . it was really tough because Eddie's waders were full of mud and made the task twice as hard. While Ed pulled the waders off, I checked Eddie's breathing. None. I opened his mouth and it was full of mud. I cleaned it out as best I could and found his throat full of mud. I thought he was dead. I reached under his neck and felt a weak pulse. That's when I decided to cut his throat and try to start him breathing again. I used my pocket knife."

Lynch's eyes bugged out. "You cut his throat?"

"I had to. I'd done this once before, in Viet Nam. I knew where to cut, but it's still hard to make yourself do it – no picnic."

"No, shit."

"I rolled Eddie onto his stomach and started giving artificial respiration by lifting and lowering his shoulders. There was a sudden gasp, a huge inhale and Eddie started breathing and choking and rasping. After a bit he seemed to be breathing evenly and we picked him up and put him in the back of my truck and rushed over here. Unbelievable, isn't it? I don't know how in hell Ed was able to get hold of Eddie, but he's one brave dude. If that rope had broken . . ."

"But it didn't break, Fred," Ed said with tears in his eyes as he returned to the waiting room. "Doc just told me that Eddie has regained consciousness and is going to make it. Hell of a deal. I think everything's going to be all right and . . . jeez, I gotta change my clothes."

Sergeant Lynch asked, "How did you get him outta the mud? How did you find him? Did you go under the mud?"

Ed ran his hands through his wet, dark curly hair and looked at Sergeant Lynch. "Just lucky," he said sucking his lower lip. "There's a peat bottom around there that's firm and is anywhere from four to twenty feet under the mud. We hit it all the time when we're putting in piles for docks and such. You gotta blow through it. Sometimes the peat's real hard. I was hoping that it wasn't too deep there and that Eddie had stopped. When I stepped into the hole I made, I sank real fast and my feet hit something . . . I hoped it was Eddie and I twisted my feet and I was able to get one foot tangled in what I hoped was his wader strap. Then I felt myself being pulled out. I was scared that my foot would slip out. What I had was heavy and I kept my eyes closed and didn't breathe and started counting and had a flash of the rope breaking and leaving us under there. When my head came out of the water, I reached down and got a good hold of Eddie."

"Damn!" Lynch said. "There could be two bodies standing upright in the mud right there in the sound and we might not have ever found them. Be there forever. Damn! You're one brave SOB. I wonder if my dad would do that for me?"

Big Ed leaned forward and touched Sergeant Lynch on the shoulder. "Oh, I think he would, cause a man's gotta do what a man's gotta do."

Chapter 2

On Mondays my wife, Jo Anne, and I eat lunch together at home, which is located on Pamlico Sound, in Hatteras Estates, in Hatteras Village, on the Outer Banks of North Carolina.

Jo Anne has her own computer consulting company and that keeps her busy most days. After I told her about the events of the morning and how we almost lost Eddie Gilliam, she allowed how we should be a hell of a lot more careful. I was about to agree when the phone rang. Jo Anne picked up the portable phone from the table, listened, asked the caller to wait just a minute, and handed it to me. She had a broad smile on her face as she said to me, "It's a woman. She's with the FBI."

"It's Bev Anderson," I said.

"Yes, it's Bev Anderson, your fantasy woman. Don't keep her waiting."

"Hello. Bev?"

"Fred," a deep soft whisper, "I had no idea that I was your fantasy girl."

"You weren't supposed to hear that. But I do think some day we should meet in person. You know, up close and personal."

She laughed. "Your wife is right there, isn't she?"

"Oh, yes. Right here and listening to every word."

"I suppose she has to keep you on a fairly short leash . . . but the primary reason I called is that 'he's b-a-a-a-c-k.'"

Bev Anderson was the number two person in the Criminal Investigative Analysis Department of the FBI. I met her last year while investigating a series of horrible murders on Hatteras Island.

"Jack Capisano?"

"Yes. And he may be heading down toward you."

"Why the devil would he come back here? Damn. What've you got?"

"We're sending a heads-up to all the local police departments in eastern North Carolina and southern Virginia because Jack's been identified as the killer of a black girl in Edenton, North Carolina. Same

M.O. as before. Only, this time he was seen. On Saturday, when he picked up the black girl, her sister saw him. She has positively identified him from the picture on our wanted flier. The headless body was left at the foot of the bridge just south of Edenton, yesterday, Sunday. Jack was driving a dark green van, but unfortunately, the sister didn't get the license number. The dead girl was young, just sixteen. It seems that he offered her twenty dollars to show him where a vet was. Had a small dog with him."

"Bev, that pick up doesn't sound like his M.O."

"No, it doesn't, but we've had four headless women's bodies reported to us recently, two in Florida, one in Georgia, and one in South Carolina. Now, this one in North Carolina. To me, two and two still make four."

"But why do you think he'll come here?"

"Because he had two misses there. That kind of thing preys on their minds. If at all possible, he'll come back to Hatteras. He'll even put himself in harm's way to do it. We've known this. We've been expecting it."

"You didn't say anything to us!"

"No, we didn't."

"Why not? Why the hell not?"

"We don't like to cause undo concern. He might

never have come back. He might not be coming back now, but I believe he is."

That was good enough for me. Bev Anderson is both an M.D. and a Ph.D. A psychiatrist who also has a Doctorate in Behavioral Science from Duke University. And she works for the FBI and she's calling me with a heads-up.

"Okay. We'll be on the lookout for a green van and I'll inform the near misses to be careful. That's why he's coming back, right?"

"Yes, and remember he's on our list for good reason."

"You mean your *Most Wanted.* Yes, we're aware of that."

"And say hello to Sheriff Tom Mathews for me. Tell him I still think about him from time to time. Goodbye and take care."

Click and she was gone. I wondered why she didn't call Matt herself for they had been summer lovers years ago. Well, maybe that's why not. According to Matt she was beautiful and she sure had a sexy voice and maybe she was my fantasy woman . . ."

"What was that all about?" Jo Anne asked with her face all scrunched up and her eyes boring a hole through me. Has Jack Capisano been seen somewhere?"

"Yes, in Edenton on Saturday, about 150 miles from here."

"Why is Ms. Anderson calling you?"

"It was just a heads-up. The Sheriff's Office is being informed. In fact all the Police Departments in eastern North Carolina are being notified. They believe he's killed again. A black teenage girl this time. Positively identified. Jack was on the FBI's ten most wanted list for interstate flight to avoid prosecution for multiple capital murder."

"Fred, I can't believe we know this guy, that he's been in our house, sat on the deck and drunk beer and told stories. And he's ugly. He's a big, ugly, terrible person."

"He's that all right."

Jack Capisano had killed a couple of women on Hatteras Island and had nearly killed two others. He stood six feet two, weighed two sixty, dark curly hair and had a huge ugly scar on his right cheek that was the result of removing a cancerous tumor and not having plastic surgery afterward. The scar looked like a burn and pulled his right eye a little out of position which is why he usually wore dark sunglasses all the time. Day and night. Yes, he was big and mean and a psycho.

"How could he believe he could ever come back here? Everyone would recognize him."

"Bev says it's part of the psycho's make up. He may want those women he didn't get before."

"Oh, Bev says that, huh? Beautiful Bev. Smart Bev. Whispering voice Bev. I'm out of here and back to work."

As Jo Anne rose from the table she added, "I heard that a hurricane has formed about two thousand miles southeast of here and is heading northwest, pointing right for us. Maybe not a hurricane, yet. More like a tropical depression but big."

"I hadn't heard that, Babe, but its chances of hitting us are slim and none if it's north of the Caribbean already. It'll turn north and northeast, they usually do, but maybe you ought to start tracking it with your computer program, anyway."

Chapter 3

A dark green van followed a black 1998 Lincoln 4x4 Navigator with Virginia plates out of the Food Lion parking lot as it turned right onto Highway 12 in the village of Avon, some fifteen miles north of Hatteras village, and proceeded south. In the new Lincoln Sport Utility Vehicle were Mr. and Mrs. J. Barton Wissenhunt of Fredericksburg, Virginia. He a successful lawyer and she the daughter of recently deceased District Judge Robert Reinhold, also of Fredericksburg.

Judge Reinhold had long been coming to Hatteras for the fishing and had been a longstanding member of the Hatteras Marlin Club. Now a decision had to be made as to whether or not the family would keep the huge, eight bedroom, modern four story rental cottage in the new upscale ocean front development called *Hatteras by the Sea*. They planned to stay a few days and make the decision. Though the cottage stayed rented some 26 weeks a year, at $3500 a week, this particular week in September was open, so they decided to break away for a few days. That morning, they had left her two teenage children with her sister and hurried south for a few days to themselves for both business and relaxation.

Married just two years, Barton felt that Sylvia spent too little time alone with him and too much time fretting over the misadventures of her spoiled twins, Jack and Jill, 14, both given to childish tantrums when not provided with instant gratification twenty-four hours a day, seven days a week, year in and year out. Slowly, he was beginning to question whether the perks outweighed the downside.

Sylvia was pert, pretty, 36, a bottle blond, trim and had been divorced a year from Army Major Ben Battle of the "Virginia Battles" when he had met her, and a year later they had married.

He, tall, slender and handsome, who had worked his way up from humble so-called white trash, an unknown father, trailer park beginnings; he who had a law degree from the University of Virginia and changed his name from Jon Barton Wissenhunt to J.

Barton Wissenhunt and was now called JB by everyone including his wife. She, who had been a Richmond debutante in 1980, the daughter of a respected judge and co-founder of the Fredericksburg Golf and Country Club, divorced with two children and a satchel of money, but unaware of his ancestry; and he, living a lie that his mother and father were killed in an automobile accident when he was four years old and was raised by a rich aunt in Ohio, unaware of Sylvia's bedroom exploits and the two abortions she had during her two-year hiatus from the marriage bed, and totally in the dark about the judge's 1996 dictum to Sylvia, "for Christ's sake, find some sonuvabitch and marry him! NOW!"

Indeed a marriage made in heaven.

Sylvia unbuckled her seat belt, took a Kleenex from her purse and turned toward her husband. "JB, do I have spittle on my blouse?"

"I'm driving, and I have a guy riding my bumper."

"JB, that man in the Food Lion sneezed and coughed all over me. I feel as though I've had a spittle shower. I feel dirty. Look at me."

A cautious man and careful driver, JB Wissenhunt looked in his rear view mirror and noticed that the van behind him had backed off his bumper, so he glanced sideways at his wife.

"You look fine. I'm certain the poor fellow didn't mean to be discourteous. In my judgment, he looked half dead. He was one sick puppy and obviously there to get medicine. He needed it."

"He looked like a hippie."

"He looked like a surfer."

"My God, JB, I've got snot in my hair! Look! What do I have to do to get you to look at me? Take off my clothes?"

"That sure wouldn't hurt."

"Yes, you'd like that wouldn't you? That's all you think about."

"Well, you know, Sylvia, if a man gets a little sugar once in a while, he doesn't think about where the bowl is."

"If you have something to say, say it!"

"I just did."

They drove in silence until they reached the Hatterasman hamburger stop in Hatteras Village, turned left at Eagle Pass Road and took the first left onto Flambeau Road which wound around to the ocean front cottages on Lighthouse Road and there turned right onto Lighthouse Road West and proceeded part way to the McDonald cul-de-sac. Just before turning left into the long driveway leading to the Reinhold cottage, which sat out like a mistaken transplant from Corolla (a very high rent yuppie summer playground settlement north of Duck), JB looked in his rear view mirror and noticed that the green van that had followed him down Route 12 was still behind him but more than a block back. Though not startled, he was surprised.

After stopping on the cement apron under the cottage, JB checked his watch, unbuckled his seat belt and turned to Sylvia. "We're here . . . it's four thirty . . . we made good time. This car certainly doesn't ride like a truck, does it? It's wonderful. Come over here and give me a kiss."

Sylvia leaned over and pecked JB on the lips. JB grabbed a breast and whispered, "Why don't you go up and get the Jacuzzi tub going in the master bedroom and I'll unload the car. Ah, unlock and take the elevator but send it back down, okay?"

"OK, the tub sounds good. Can you handle all our stuff?"

"Can I handle it? You have to ask? I wonder if there's cold beer here?"

"JB, the house has been rented. I wouldn't count on it or on anything else."

By ten to five, JB had completed the unloading and was standing in the large country kitchen putting away groceries when the doorbell rang. He looked up at the balcony overlooking the kitchen and dining room and yelled out, "Can you get that, Honey?"

"I can't, I'm undressed," Sylvia yelled back.

JB could hear the large blue tub filling in the room over him. "OK. I'll get it. Who the heck could it be anyway?"

"Maybe it's the realtor or maybe it's a neighbor."

"I'll check."

JB walked down a floor and opened the front door. A large dark haired man wearing sunglasses stood facing him on the porch. JB unlatched the storm door, pushed it open and asked, "Can I help you?"

"Are you Judge Reinhold?"

The stranger was wearing a Carolina Panthers T-shirt and black trousers and looked vaguely familiar to JB. "Why do you ask?"

"I seen the name on the cottage. Judge and Catherine Reinhold from Fredericksburg, Virginia. I'm from the phone company. We got a complaint that the phone was out of order. Is it?"

"We just arrived here so I really don't know."

"You a renter?"

"Ah, no . . . this house is owned by my father-in-law."

"Is he here?"

"No, just my wife and me."

"Are you staying long?"

"A few days. Why do you ask?"

"Why don't you check the phone?"

JB began to feel uneasy. "Yes, I will. One minute, please." He shut the storm door and the front door and left the telephone man on the porch. The nearest phone was in the kitchen on the bar, so he hurried up to the kitchen and picked up the receiver. No dial tone. He set it down and hurried back to the door.

"We have no dial tone . . . I don't see your truck. Where is it?"

"It's parked under the house."

"Do you have some identification? I mean you aren't exactly dressed like a telephone man."

"Yessir, I have all the identification I need right here." The telephone man reached back with his right hand as though reaching for his wallet and unsheathed a large Buck knife hanging from his belt. As he stepped forward, he opened the knife and then grabbed JB by the throat with his left hand. With his right, he swung the huge knife up and plunged it under JB's sternum. With a twist, he destroyed the heart muscle. He held JB up while he died and then dropped him in the foyer. With his foot on JB's stomach, he retrieved his knife, shut the storm door, then shut and locked the front door.

Suddenly, a woman's voice yelled out from somewhere in the house. "JB, do I need to get dressed?"

Chapter 4

Sylvia Wissenhunt woke with a start when a strong masculine hand began stroking her body. It was dark. Then, she remembered. She was on the bed in the master bedroom where she had been put yesterday afternoon. She could feel that her wrists were still tied to the headboard and her feet still tied to the foot of the bed. She was nude lying on her stomach spread eagle. Her chin was on a pillow and the position had given her a stiff, sore neck. She felt hot as though she had a fever and her mouth was dry. She could feel the tape covering her lips pulling on her face. She wanted a drink of water. When she was little, she would awake and want water, and she'd call out and mother would bring it. But this was different.

Sylvia was terrified, but she made no sound or movement as the hand again started at her head and stroked down through her hair and over her neck, down her back and stopped before rising up over her bottom. The hand rubbed in a circle and then rose up and eased between her buttocks and stopped on her thigh. Then, it did it again and again and again. She wanted to scream but she couldn't. She wanted to cry but she didn't. She lay thinking and praying and trying to keep the images of yesterday from flooding back.

In her mind's eye she could see the horrible man who had hurt her husband and walked into her bedroom as she was coming out of the bathroom with just her robe on. The big dark haired ugly man had crossed the room fast and had thrust a huge knife up under her chin. He hadn't cut her but he said he would and he also said that he had already sent her husband *to the other side*. What did that mean? It meant that JB was dead, that's what it meant, but she didn't want to accept it. She couldn't accept it. JB or Daddy would save her. Daddy would come and rescue her with the FBI and the State Police. Daddy would know something was wrong and hurry down from Fredericksburg. But Daddy had died. DADDY DIED!

Sylvia felt the hand slide into her buttocks again

and linger for a while then move on and rest on her thigh. She began to feel hollow, sick to her stomach. She did a dry heave and it frightened her. She could choke on vomit. She was going to die. This crude man was going to kill her.

Then, a sudden burst of energy. She'd fight! She wasn't going to lie down and die. Whatever it took, she would survive. She made a pledge that she'd do whatever it took. She shut her eyes tightly and swore to herself that she would live for the sake of the children. Whatever horrible things she had to do with this man, she would do. Anything. Then, she settled herself and tried to stop the churning in her stomach.

The hand turned her head onto her cheek and pinched her nose shut. Sylvia's cheeks caved in and she couldn't breathe. She tried to move her head but the hand was strong and held her. She squirmed on the bed and rolled her eyes. She screamed in her throat, but she couldn't break away from the hand. She could feel herself blacking out and she tried to come to her knees, but could not. A low animal growl came from her throat and then she could breathe. He had let go.

She took two deep breaths and closed her teary eyes.

"You didn't think that I knew you were awake,

but I did." The voice was deep and soft and wasn't at all threatening. Sylvia thought it was a nice voice, not that of a killer. Not the voice of someone who had hurt her husband. She relaxed a little as the hand started again to stroke her body and then stiffened when the hand stopped on her buttocks.

"You have nice hair, Sylvia, not sticky like so many women. Not filled with spray, but long and soft. I'd untape you're mouth but I think you'd talk or scream and I really don't like how you sound, Sylvia. Too much accent. This is better. If you screamed then I'd have to hurt you, so I won't do that. And if I took the tape off, I couldn't easily show you that I control your life."

The hand went back to her nose and pinched.

"You see Sylvia, now you can't breathe and now you can, and now you can't and now you can."

Suddenly, he started humming *Raindrops* and pinching Sylvia's nose in rhythm with his humming.

"Remember, Sylvia, I'm your master and you're my slave, forever and ever. Amen."

He got up from the bed and moved away. She heard him in the bathroom. Water running. He returned and turned on the bedside light. She saw his face close to hers. He was smiling and she stared at the huge scar on his cheek. She looked into his eyes and they were dark brown and appeared soft like a puppy's. His face was near hers. She could smell his minted breath.

"Sylvia, I hate the name Sylvia. I like Karen. I like Susan, too. I'll call you Karen. No more Sylvia, only Karen . . . and when you speak, you must always whisper, Karen. I like that. I like it very much. I've brought you some water, Karen, and I'm going to remove the tape. If you scream or talk above a whisper, I'll cut your throat." He chuckled, "Just like your man. I cut his throat, you know. Ear to ear, Karen." He chuckled again. "He's gone to the other side with two big smiles. One on his face and one under his chin. Lordy, he bled a lot, Karen. It took me a while to clean up downstairs, but it's nice and clean, now. It's as though he was never here. He never existed. There's just you and me."

He tore the tape off Sylvia's mouth and forced the glass to her lips and she raised her head and tried to drink and began choking. He stopped and waited, then gave her some more water, spilling most of it onto the pillow.

"My name's Jack, Karen. Wet your lips good, drink deeply, Karen, and call me Jack. Wet your mouth. I'm going to kiss you, my sweet."

Suddenly, the light went off and Sylvia smelled

his breath again. He whispered, "Say Jack. Go ahead and say it."

"Jack," she whispered from a sore throat.

"Say it again."

"Jack."

Then she felt his lips on hers and he forced his tongue into her mouth. Slowly, he sucked her tongue into his mouth and began breathing hard. He stopped and pulled away. "Karen, Karen," he whispered, "You're hot. I can feel it. You're my favorite, now. The others can't kiss like you do, Karen. Next to you, they're just cold soft skin and hair. But you, Love, are warm. My search may be over. Kiss me again, Karen, slow and wet."

Chapter 5

By ten o'clock Tuesday morning, Ed and I had finished the bulkhead work we had started yesterday and were about half through unloading my truck and putting the tools and pump and other equipment away in the garage. Ed looked as though he hadn't gotten much sleep last night. His usual outgoing nature was muffled. He seemed deep in thought. As is usual with men, we hadn't talked about the accident. When and if he wanted to talk about it, he would. So far, he hadn't.

Ed was coiling a long electrical extension cord around his elbow and thumb and he stopped, shook his head and looked at me. "You just never know, do you?"

"Nope." I said.

"You know, Fred, right now my son could be dead. Lost in the mud. Trudy and me, our life would be in shambles, and we couldn't really even put up a headstone. Where would we put it? And every time I came out here, I'd be wondering about . . . I guess we'd a gotten a back hoe and dug him out. Maybe not. Could have been real deep. Makes you wonder."

I knew young Eddie wasn't married and lived at home. He had divorced several years back from a teenager he'd impregnated. Now, I understood, she had three or four kids with two or three fathers and lived up the road in Avon.

"Where is Eddie, now?" I asked.

"Home in bed. Gonna be all right. Got a hole in his neck that hasta heal, and he's got some water in his chest that's causing pleurisy and he's getting some medicine for that. But he's safe and sound. Yessir, thank God. He's safe and sound. I have to tell you, though, I couldn't cut him like you did. Thanks."

"Had to be done. Did it before. But you know, since that happened, and I guess really whenever I think about death, I always seem to recall something I once saw here in the Village. It was on one of those church billboards, you know the kind out in front of the church. It was like the thought for the day and it said 'DO YOU WANT TO GO TO HEAVEN BY YOURSELF OR TO HELL WITH YOUR FRIENDS?' I've always thought the preacher had it backwards, but it makes you stop and think, doesn't it?"

"That was Reverend Packard's message. I saw it. He's a smart man. You best pay attention."

From working with Ed, I knew that he was a storm freak. His family, the Gilliams, had been on the Outer Banks for more than a hundred years, since just after the Civil War. He knew about the really terrible storms and the small ones. In fact he was a walking encyclopedia on hurricanes and nor'easters.

"I've heard that there's a storm coming, Ed. You know anything about it?" I turned my head and grimaced because for just a second I'd forgotten that this was like asking a preacher if he knew anything about God.

He frowned. "There's an advisory out. Could be bad." Then he grinned as though a weight had been lifted from his soul.

"Think so? Why do you say that?"

"In 19 and 33, a hurricane came straight across the Atlantic, no turns, no nothing. Straight northwest. Hit right at Buxton. The eye went right over the lighthouse. Winds were about 110 miles per hour, a big surge. This one looks to me to be like it. The 19 and 33 storm did some damage, but not as bad as Emily in 1993 . . . You know, all this comes from Africa."

Here we go. "I've heard that."

"It's true. There's about fifty tropical disturbances that come out of West Africa each year and half develop into tropical depressions."

"What's the difference between a disturbance and a depression?" I asked.

"A disturbance is a hot flow of air from Africa that has no front, be like a circle, and it's several hundred miles across. It's like it has a center and some flow of air. Has to stay like that for twenty-four hours."

Ed was warming to the subject.

"Now, a tropical depression is a cyclone that has wind speed of less than 38 miles per hour. It's a real storm, but a small one.

"Of those depressions, about ten become tropical storms, which means that the winds get over 38 and stay less than 73 miles per hour. Of those storms, six become hurricanes with winds over 74. So, the chances of a disturbance becoming a hurricane is . . ."

"One in eight?"

Ed smiled. "Yeah. About one in eight. Do you know the worst?"

"Worst, how? Killed the most people? Costliest? Strongest?"

"All them. Deadliest was in 1900. Killed 6,000 people in Houston, Texas. Might have been as high as 10-12 thousand people . . . maybe it wasn't Houston . . . maybe it was in Galveston. Worst disaster in American history. Worse than the San Francisco earthquake or the Chicago fire. You wouldn't expect it there. Yeah. It was Galveston. I remember, now.

"The costliest was Andrew, in 1992. Broke all the insurance companies. Winds of 140 to 150, hit Florida and crossed it and went into the Gulf of Mexico and hit the Gulf Coast somewhere. It was the third strongest storm to ever hit the U.S. The strongest storm was in 1935 and it killed 500 people when it hit the Florida Keys. Winds were better than 160. This new one of ours is called Dixie, and this morning it was 1200 miles east southeast of Hatteras, and the winds were up to 86 miles an hour . . . that makes it a hurricane, already . . . and it was moving at 14 miles an hour, and that's more than 300 miles a day. Could be here in four days."

"Could and probably will turn north," I said.

"Could turn north, but it won't," he said.

I shook my head. "How do you know all this?"

Ed smiled from ear to ear and broke out a crushed pack of Winstons from his shirt pocket. He wiggled his Zippo lighter from the watch pocket in his Levis and lit up. He blew out a strong puff of smoke from his mouth and nose, still smiling. "I just try to keep up. A man's gotta have a hobby. It keeps his pump primed."

Outer Bankers love to drink, and I'm a banker, and it was five-fifteen, so I was drinking while sitting on my deck chatting with Jo Anne, who is not nationally known as a teetotaler, and is known to wet her whistle now and again if asked politely.

I was twisting my glass and admiring the dark rich color of the Johnnie Walker Black while it hosted a few ice cubes when Amos leaped from where he was sleeping at my feet and ran barking from the deck. Obviously, someone had arrived on or near my property.

"Amos! Get back over here!" I shouted to an empty deck. The barking stopped, signaling that Amos knew the visitor. Shortly, the dog returned with Sheriff Mathews in tow. Amos likes Matt and Matt was rubbing Amos' head as they crossed the deck. Amos was wagging his tail and pleased with himself.

"Hello, Matt. Sit down. Can I buy you a drink?"

Sheriff Matt is a tall, lanky fellow, with dark hair, turning gray, and reminds you of Fred MacMurray from the old TV show *My Three Sons.* He never wears a uniform, or at least I've never seen him in one. In the winter he usually wears a camel sportcoat over a white shirt and gray slacks. The rest of the year he wears a white short sleeved shirts with the gray slacks. Today was short sleeve day. And always, he wears a gray Stetson.

Matt's never been married, has a girl friend in Buxton, another one in Manteo, used to be a Charter Boat Captain, and is well thought of and respected throughout the county, except maybe for several County Commissioners, who think he has too large a budget and is overpaying his under-paid deputies, of whom I am one, though I don't get paid at all.

I'm a special deputy, with special meaning that I receive no money, no allowances, no uniform, no car, no ticket book, can't carry a weapon, report only to Matt, and am thought of as a fifth wheel by most of the deputies. But I do have a badge. So, why do I do it? Because Matt asked me to, that's why, and if that's good enough for me, it's good enough for you.

"Thanks for the offer, Fred, but I'll pass on the drink. Hello, Jo Anne, sorry to break in on your evening like this but it seems the shit has hit the proverbial fan."

"You mean about Capisano being seen in Edenton, Matt?" I asked.

"Well, that's part of it. But there's a whole lot worse."

"What's worse than that sonuvabitch?"

Matt slipped into an empty wooden deck chair and thought for a minute or two. Satisfied, he turned to Jo Anne and said, "Jo Anne, you must not repeat what I'm about to say . . . we may have an outbreak of the plague here in the village that could wipe us all out and . . . and a massive hurricane is headed our way, hell, right for us, and we have a serial killer running around the island somewhere. How's that for a Tuesday afternoon in September? You know, Fred. I will take a drink. A tall one. Mostly scotch. Thanks."

I got up and hurried to the kitchen, poured a tall Johnnie with more water and ice than *we* use, added a little Johnnie to my glass and hurried back outside. I handed the drink to Matt with a napkin and as I retook my seat I noticed that Jo Anne was noticing that my glass was fuller than hers. Caught, I winked at her and ignored her plight. Matt had my full attention.

"Yo, Matt! We know about the storm and the possibility that Capisano is somewhere about, but what the hell is this about the plague? Are you talking about the black plague?"

Matt took a long drink, swallowed, and grimaced a little. "It still tastes like kerosene." He grinned. "Course good, expensive kerosene. You ask black plague, blue plague, who the devil knows? Here's the story. This afternoon about two o'clock a young man is brought into the Medical Center by two friends. It seems that they're here windsurfing from Patterson, New Jersey. Friday, the three young fellows, all in their twenties, rented a cottage in Frisco, there on the left going north just before you get to the Quarterdeck Restaurant."

"Nice but not cheap," I said.

"No, not cheap. But those cottages are used a lot by groups of surfers, and more recently by windsurfers as well, because they're right on the sound. One of the boys, Tom Kerry, took sick on Saturday. At first they thought he had the flu because he had a fever and chills and muscle aches and fatigue and all that. He stayed in bed on Sunday, but got sicker and started swelling under his arms. They were going to take him to the Medical Center on Monday because he was

coughing, but at the last minute he decided he
didn't want to go, so they took him to the Food
Lion in Avon, where they picked up groceries and
Kerry bought some over-the-counter stuff and a
thermometer. He felt that he had the flu, and they
were down for the week, so they didn't feel rushed.
His temperature was 102 to 103, so they discussed
their options, and they fed him aspirin and Tylenol
. . . but Monday night he started coughing up blood
and his arm pits and groin were turning black, so
the boys called 911 and got an ambulance. This was
about two or three this morning. On site, the
paramedics described to Doctor Allen what they had
and he ordered them to put on surgical masks right
then and there. Then, Kerry was taken to the
Medical Center and Doctor Allen met them there.

"As soon as Doctor Allen saw young Kerry, he
isolated him. Doc's using one of the examining
rooms for isolation. He then sent the paramedics
back after the other two boys. When he examined
them, he found that they too had fevers and chills
and were developing a cough. So Doc's isolated
them and has all of them on some kind of drugs."

"Is he sure it's the plague?" I asked.

"He sure thinks it is. He checked the bacteria
under a microscope, and he said it sure looked like
plague because plague bacteria are very different

looking. He said they look like closed safety pins. He's running a culture to be sure as we speak, but it takes a day or two. He's also called the Center for Disease Control in Atlanta. They're sending some people here soonest, so they must think he's onto something."

Jo Anne looked frightened. "Do they know if he got it here on the island or somewhere else, Matt?" she asked.

"Doc's interviewed young Kerry and his two friends. According to him, he didn't get much from them. Kerry isn't making much sense."

I said, "I don't know much about the plague, but I think that it comes from fleas on rats and the rats have to be in a filthy environment . . . and the fleas have to bite people. I know plague is a bacteria, so I think it has to be passed from person to person by touching a sore or something like that. It has to get into the blood stream, kind of like HIV, maybe."

"Not according to Doc. He says if it gets too bad and gets in the lungs, you can pass it along, you know, spread it by coughing."

Jo Anne said, "My God, has this guy, Kerry, been around a lot of people?"

"Well, we know he went to the Food Lion on Monday, and he was coughing then. Saturday, he went windsurfing with his friends and had lunch and dinner at the Quarterdeck. Sunday he didn't leave the house. That's about it."

"Could there be rats in the house they rented?" Jo Anne asked.

"Could be," Matt said. "In fact that's one reason I'm here. Doctor Allen wants us to take a look around the rental cottage and report back to him."

I jumped up. "Who's us, Matt? You mean you and me?"

"Yes."

"Hey, I'm not for entering a house where there's been plague, for heaven's sake. Are you?"

"The doc says we'll be safe if we wear surgical masks and spray ourselves with an insect repellent before we go in."

Jo Anne's eyes were flashing. "Fred's not going anywhere near that house, and you shouldn't be asking him to. There may be plague fleas all over the place."

"Doc doesn't think so. According to him and a talk he had with CDC in Atlanta, if Kerry has the plague, and remember, he may not, he had to get it by an infected flea bite, touching a sore on someone who has it and is broken out with an open sore, or by breathing in bacteria from the cough of someone who is very infected with plague. None of these things are probable."

"Well, he got it from somewhere!" Jo Anne shouted. "And what you're leading up to but not saying is that if the plague is here, and is being spread around by coughing, then everyone in the village could end up with it. That's right, isn't it?"

"Not if we're careful, but it is a possibility."

"And you and Fred are going to go snooping around the house where these boys stayed and look for what?"

"Well, first we're going to interview the two other boys and . . ."

"Matt! They've got it too, don't they? You said they were sick and now quarantined. How are you going to interview them?"

"Very carefully, Jo Anne. Very carefully, indeed."

Chapter 6

Matt and I arrived at the Medical Center at five minutes to six that evening. We drove separately the mile and a half from my home. As I sat alone for those few minutes in my truck, I couldn't keep my mind off what was happening and what might lie ahead. Did we have an outbreak of a most dreaded disease on Hatteras Island? Could I catch the plague from these guys? I recalled that just before I shipped out for Viet Nam, back in 1965, I was given two shots some two weeks apart to immunize me from the plague. As I recalled, the first shot made me sick, in fact, bedridden sick. Of course I didn't catch the plague over there, but come to think of it, I didn't recall anyone there catching the plague. I made up my mind right then and there that I'd get myself a plague shot before I had anything to do with this investigation. Boy, was I wrong.

Upon arrival at the Medical Center we tried the emergency side door and found it locked. We scurried around to the front door and found it locked, too. Our pounding on the door eventually brought Doctor Allen, Doctor Porter Hardy, Head Nurse Susan Wyche and RN Wendy Price to the waiting room and an eventual door opening. All were wearing green scrubs, rubber gloves and surgical masks, much like you see on the TV show *ER*.

First order of business was to give Matt and me surgical masks. We put them on, and the act of doing it brought on a feeling of gloom and doom, as though we were in the middle of an *X-Files* episode.

Doctor Hardy's slightly muffled voice requested that we all sit down. Without being told, we arranged our chairs in a circle. "Tom Kerry is dead," Doctor Hardy said in a soft voice. "He died just a few minutes ago."

"That was awfully fast, wasn't it?" I asked.

Doctor Hardy leaned back in his chair and crossed his arms over his chest in a very defensive position. "I'm going to keep this simple. We believe he died of pneumonic plague, which means that it settled in his chest, and also means that it is the absolute worst kind, for it can be transferred from person to person by coughing or even just breathing in and out. To answer your question, Fred, no, it's not fast for pneumonic plague. That form is very virulent. His two friends sharing the cottage are also infected. We're treating them both with large doses of streptomycin and we're hopeful, but . . . the big question is, how much of this is out in the community?

"We've learned that the boys arrived on Friday evening and had pizza delivered, stayed in Friday night. Only contact was with the pizza delivery man, or in this case, women from the Gingerbread House. That's who delivered. Saturday, all three went windsurfing off the beach near their cottage, and had lunch at the Quarterdeck. They windsurfed in the afternoon, but Kerry started feeling ill and he stopped around three o'clock . . . he went inside and fell asleep on the couch. He slept until around six when the other boys woke him and they drank beer until seven then all three went to the Quarterdeck for dinner. They made several contacts there . . . and might have been carrying the bacteria on hands or elsewhere . . . but perhaps they weren't then contagious. Sunday, Kerry stayed in bed all day, and the other two windsurfed and made lunch at the cottage and went to Gary's Restaurant for dinner. Were they then carrying the bacteria? Good question. Kerry drank water and beer, Sunday, ate nothing, never left the cottage."

Matt said, "Since those two weren't feeling bad, we can assume they weren't contagious, right?"

Doctor Hardy scratched himself on the sleeve wearing the gloves, and the action seemed peculiar. "That's probably right, Sheriff, but they may have been carrying the bacteria on their clothes or on their hands and contaminated door knobs, dishes, all manner of things. We don't know."

The doctor went on. "Monday, we have a real problem. All three men went to the Food Lion and had contact with lots of people and Kerry might have been very contagious then. They could have left bacteria all over the grocery store. It has to be the absolute last place in the world we would want those guys to be running around. That little trip could turn out to be just disastrous for the island. As you know, Matt, we've been in contact with CDC in Atlanta, and they're sending an investigator to look at the cases, look for more cases, interview patients, take lab samples, and report back to Atlanta. Doctor Allen has been in contact with CDC and he's handling the lab chemistry on our end throughout this ordeal."

The telephone rang and Nurse Wendy hurried through the double doors to answer. Seconds later she called from the receptionist's window that CDC was on the phone and they wanted to talk to Doctor Allen. Tom Allen ran from the room.

Sheriff Mathews stood and began pacing. "Porter, what you're telling us is that we may have a serious epidemic about to break out here. Am I right about that?"

"Yes, you are. But this may be isolated and we may only have a few cases or perhaps we've already seen the worst of what we'll have."

"Do you really believe that, Doc?" I asked.

"No, I don't . . . well, maybe. I just don't know."

"Are we going to have to isolate the island?" I asked.

"Interesting you should bring that up, Fred," Doctor Allen said as he reentered the waiting room.

We all looked to him.

"With Kerry's death and the other two boys sick, CDC wants us to immediately isolate the island, and their investigator, Doctor Joan Savage, will arrive by CDC jet at the air strip just before dark. Probably quarter to eight or so. I told them not to be late for we only have a daylight airport . . . and they

said that they knew that. They're also sending
several thousand units of plague vaccine and
antibiotic supplies of streptomycin and tetracycline.
They want all Public Health and Public Safety
personnel to start personal preventive measures as
soon as the drugs arrive and we're to start island
wide inoculations as soon as we can get set up.
Well, that ought to keep us busy . . . So, Sheriff,
how do we shut down the island and at the same
time prevent sensationalism and panic? And, by the
way, CDC also said that they have discussed the
situation with the Governor's Office and their
instructions were to do whatever has to be done to
contain the problem and that we would be most
cooperative."

Matt grimaced. "Well, I must say it's about time
someone cut me in. Dammit, I'll have the
governor's men all over my ass and . . . I suppose
I'll have to assign someone just to keep them up to
speed. Bullshit! . . ."

The sheriff looked around and we all looked at
the floor. "Okay, here's the plan. I'll personally
work with the state police and set up the road
block at the Bonner Bridge. Only one state cop
lives on the island, so I'll need more assigned on
a permanent basis until these crises are over.
Obviously they can't leave either. No one on, no

one off . . . this will cause real problems. Problems we can't even begin to address now. I'll also see to stopping the ferries to Ocracoke. If O-cokers want to leave, they'll have to go the other way to Swan Quarter or Cedar Island."

Nurse Susan asked, "What about the hurricane? What if we have to evacuate the island? How are we going to do that?"

Matt glared at Susan. "We aren't. The short answer is that we aren't. If the hurricane hits while we're quarantined, we all stay here. And I don't want to think about that right now. Dare County Emergency Management has to be notified and this is going to drive them nuts because they already have a full plate. Fred, you stay put for now, and I'll send my Lieutenant Randy Howard over here later. I want you to work with the Medical Center and be the go-between with them and Public Safety. I guess the first order of business is to set up inoculations."

Doctor Tom Allen raised his hand. It suddenly occurred to me how strange we all looked with our masks and I smiled but no one knew it. "I think our first order of business," Doc Tom said, "is the contaminated body in room three. What do we do with it?"

"Any ideas?" Matt asked.

"We either got to bury it or freeze it," I volunteered.

"I don't see burying," Doctor Hardy offered. "That leaves freezing. Where do we do that?"

"Where's a big freezer?" I asked.

Nurse Wendy: "Restaurants. Channel Bass has a big one, but I'm sure it's full of food."

"Fishhouses?" I said. "That's it, fishhouses."

Matt violently shook his head. "No! That'll contaminate the fishhouse,"

"We'll just have to worry that later, Matt. Go ahead. Take off. I'll take care of things here. And my first order of business is to get hold of Tim Midgett. We're going to need some real estate clout and a community relations guy and I vote for him."

"Good choice! I'll have my office get ahold of everyone we can . . . who's on the island . . . in Public Safety and Public Health and all the volunteer outfits. Fire, Rescue, LCDR Stephens for the Coast Guard Group, State Police, Park Service Rangers, Fisheries, Emergency Planning, and on and on. Meeting at nine o'clock tonight at . . . where? Where's big enough?"

"The Civic Center?" Doc Tom Allen asked.

"Good, perfect. Be there."

Chapter 7

I was standing near the doors of the Civic Center when Doctor Tom Allen rose to speak. It was nine-thirty and we had a full house and so far, we had only heard from Sheriff Matt who informed the room that we had a man die of the plague today and that we were here to take early action to ensure that we had no epidemic. He had been bombarded with questions, many of which he couldn't answer. The one I thought really struck a bell was the last one from a female rescue volunteer who asked if we weren't all really taking a big gamble by meeting here, in this room, at this time under these circumstances. Matt stared at her for a few seconds and quickly turned the meeting over to Doctor Allen.

Doctor Allen introduced Doctor Joan Savage, the CDC investigator. She was 30 something, short, stocky, had dark hair, cut short and mannish, small and dark piercing eyes behind large owlish glasses. She had thick ankles and was dressed in a blue high water pants suit that exaggerated the size of her behind, and she wore comfortable shoes. Rings on all fingers, luckily no bells on her toes, and a clipboard under her arm completed her accessories. Definitely all business but not show business. As promised by the CDC, she had brought vaccine and drugs on the plane with her. The plane stayed long enough to land, unload, and take off. I met her, rushed her to the Medical Center where she met the "doctor in charge" and made it quite clear that her first order of business was to ascertain whether or not we had a "true" plague death. She pointed out that the Hatteras Medical staff didn't have the experience to make that call. Our family doctors took offense, and Doc Allen read her the riot act and then offered that he was always interested in a second opinion or, in this case, a third opinion even though he and Doctor Hardy were certain about the bacteria.

As reported to me, "She looked, she confirmed Kerry died of the plague, and agreed we had a big problem with two plague stricken men in isolation and a possible epidemic at hand, and was hopeful we could trace the origin of the bacteria and then mumbled something about never knowing what to expect in the far flung rural areas, blah, blah, blah . . ."

Doctor Allen was wearing his white coat which made him look very doctorish but not his surgical mask. As the noise level grew in the room he waved his hands and quieted everyone. "Folks, let me explain what we're up against. First, what is plague? Plague is a serious illness caused by bacteria called *Yersinia pestis.* The disease is carried by rodents such as rats and mice and their fleas, which can transmit the disease to humans as well as other animals. Actually, plague is very rare in the United States, but cases are still reported in the southwestern states of New Mexico, Arizona, Colorado, Nevada and California. The most common form of plague is bubonic which affects the body's lymph nodes. When or if the disease involves the lungs, it's called pneumonic plague and that's the worst kind as far as we're concerned.

"Some of you may recall in school studying the so-called *Black Death* or *Black Plague* that swept the world in the thirteen hundreds. That was mainly bubonic plague which swells the lymph nodes and turns them black. Thus, the *Black Plague.*

"That plague was commonly spread through fleas that had made a meal from chewing on a rat, and the ingested plague bacteria would multiply in the flea's upper digestive system and eventually obstruct it. When the flea feeds again on a human or another rodent, the obstruction causes the freshly ingested blood to be regurgitated back into the bite, along with the plague bacteria. The circulatory system of the bitten individual then carries the bacteria throughout the body. Are there any questions so far?"

The room stayed quiet.

"None? Okay . . . to continue . . . in our southwest, the plague is carried by, or better, I should say is usually carried by rock squirrels. And remember something. A squirrel is really nothing but a kinda rat, a rodent, with a fancy tail. The last recorded rat-borne epidemic in the U.S., rat-to-people and then people-to-people, was in Los Angeles in 1924 . . . and in those several hundred cases, thirty-two became pneumonic plague and thirty-one of those folks died. No one who had just bubonic plague died. Which means the bacteria were killed before they infected the lungs. Since 1924, we've had about sixteen cases a year in the U.S., and just about all were connected to rock squirrels or ground squirrels and their fleas. But we haven't seen any human infection to the east of the Mississippi River, even though prairie dogs, deer mice, wood rats, and chipmunks occasionally serve as sources of human infection, as well as wild rabbits, deer and antelope all of whom can get infected when there is a wild rodent outbreak. Hell, even domestic cats and dogs can become infected from fleas or from eating wild rodents and thus bring plague into the house. If that happens, you may become infected and perhaps even infect someone else."

An attractive, bleached blond, middle-aged woman I didn't recognize stood up and said, "Doctor Allen, what you're saying is scaring me to death. Are you saying that if we have pneumonic plague here on the island, and it gets around, that we're all going to die? Is that what you're really saying?"

CDC's Joan Savage jumped to her feet. "Doctor Allen, I'll take that question. Ma'am, what he's saying is that if the plague gets out of control, and we're here to control it, many people will die. From a start right here, it could sweep up and down the east coast and push out into the midwest and all the way to the west coast. Thousands, even millions could die. But that's why we have the Centers for Disease Control and Prevention now headquartered in Atlanta, Georgia. That's why we have trained, competent, investigators, like myself, come to hot areas to stop epidemics before they start. You asked if Doctor Allen was trying to scare you, I don't think so. I think that he's trying to educate you about this terrible, terrible disease. And through all our efforts, we'll find the origins of this outbreak on Hatteras Island."

"Thank you, Doctor Savage. Would you like to take up where I left off?" Doctor Allen said through a phony smile. I was certain it pained him to no end to thank Joan Savage for anything and his little barb showed that he knew she was going to be looking over his shoulder and be a thorn in his side as long as she was here. It appeared that Doctor Hardy had indeed taken the high road by passing on the opportunity to work closely with Doctor Savage who seemed to hold the practice of family medicine just slightly above the practice of voodoo. Though it is generally accepted in the field of medicine that family practitioners are the best trained and have broader experiences than any other branch of medicine, "cause they borne ya and they bury ya," many over-educated-arrogant-medical-buffoons find it pleasing to their egos to attempt to denigrate the family doctor's contribution to effective health care.

Doctor Savage shook her head violently. "No, no, Doctor Allen, you're doing just fine."

"Thank you very much, Doctor Savage. Folks, you ask are we trying to scare you a little? Yes, I suppose we are. But only so we will all do the best job we can. As I was saying, the pneumonic plague is the most dangerous form, because it invades the victim's lungs and they fill with frothy, bloody liquid and the disease can be spread through aerosol droplets released through coughs, sneezes, or fluid contact. It can also become a secondary result of untreated bubonic plague. Although usually not as common as bubonic, it is much more deadly. So, it's important that we identify victims as early as possible. If not, it's 'Katy bar the door.' If left untreated, the mortality rate for pneumonic plague is right at 100%, as compared to untreated bubonic at about 50% dead.

"To put all this in perspective, plague killed about 25% of the population of Europe in the 1300's or some 25 million people . . . that's more than the population of North Carolina, Virginia, West Virginia, Maryland and Delaware combined. The absolute worst plague epidemic ever recorded came out of Egypt around 550 AD, and swept across the Middle East, Europe, and Asia, killing an estimated 100 million people. That particular plague is important to note not just for the number of deaths, but it was more than likely the more virulent pneumonic form and was quickly passed from person to person. Thus, the very high mortality rate."

"Yeah, Doc, but that was all a long time ago," from a uniformed Park Ranger. I thought it might be my friend Allen Pinkerton but he didn't stand up so I couldn't be sure. "Now we have modern medicine and all that. What's it got to do with us?"

"I'll tell you what it's got to do with us. We just had a young man die of the plague in less than three days and more than likely about twenty-four hours after it became pneumonic. And we started treating two young men this morning for plague with antibiotics. Thus, far we've seen no improvement. Of course it's early, but we should have already seen a change in the blood. We haven't. Believe me, that's not good."

Doctor Allen stopped and looked around the room. "I'm not here to cause a panic, especially with you folks, since you're the ones who must contain it. CDC is here to help us. In fact they're in charge. Remember that! They are in charge. Now, back to some more history. This time a little closer to our time frame. In 1980, there were some 18 plague cases in the United States, and most occurred in kids under 20. All were treated and three died. That's one in six dead and all had bubonic plague, not pneumonic. We believe the high death rate was due to immature immune systems in the kids under 18.

"In September 1984, there was an epidemic in India and the CDC put the whole North American continent on alert for pneumonic plague because people from India traveling by aircraft might be carrying the disease. None was discovered, but the whole continent went on alert. That's what we're playing with here. For your information, CDC has already notified all the medical facilities on the east coast to be alert for plague symptoms. We don't know where these boys picked this up but we do know that one was very sick when he visited the Food Lion on Monday. That was yesterday. He's now dead. His companions are in critical condition. There were many people in the Food Lion on Monday. Some of them could be infected. We just don't know, yet. But as you do know, as of tonight, this island is under quarantine.

"Now, I want to again go over how this disease is transmitted . . . from animal-to-animal and from animal-to-human by bites from infected fleas. Occasionally, the bacteria enter through a break in the skin by direct contact with tissue or body fluids of a plague-infected animal . . . ah, like from skinning a rabbit, or dressing out a deer, or even tending to an infected person. Primary plague pneumonia is transmitted by inhaling infected droplets that are expelled by the coughing of a person or animals, especially cats, who are infected with pneumonic plague."

From the back of the room, "So, you're saying animals get the pneumonic plague and can give it to you? And not just from fleas?"

"That's correct. I've got to tell you that transmission of bubonic plague from person-to-person is uncommon, even rare, and hasn't been seen in the United States since that time I mentioned before, in 1924, in Los Angeles. Usually, one person gets bubonic plague, they're treated and hopefully survive and it never becomes pneumonic and is not passed on. It's contained. So, we don't have much experience with plague epidemics, and we don't want to gain it here.

"I'm going to give you some information on diagnosis and treatment . . . and you may ask what the hell do I need this for, and I'm telling you so you better understand what we as a community are going to do. The better informed we are, the faster we're going to defeat this problem.

"The first symptoms of bubonic plague are sudden fever with painful swelling of the lymph nodes . . ."

"What's a lymph node and where is it?"

"Good question. A lymph node is a lymph gland, and it's part of your immune system for fighting infections. They're right here on your neck . . . can everybody see that? . . . okay, they are also in the arm pits, and in the groin area, here and here. They'll swell and get painful, fill with pus, turn black and infect the entire body through the blood stream. Blood vessels break causing internal bleeding and dried blood under the skin turns black, and thus, the name *Black Plague* or *Black Death*. There'll also be chills, muscle-aches, weakness, fatigue, nausea and headaches. If the infection spreads to the lungs, it produces pneumonia that is highly contagious, and as we said earlier, it is usually fatal. Pneumonic plague is characterized by high fever, maybe 104 to 105 degrees, again swelling of the lymph nodes, cough, chest pain and blood in the saliva, bloody sputum. Remember, once in the lungs, it's deadly, both to the victim and you. Victims are going to have to be isolated. More than likely isolated by people in Public Health and Public Safety. You folks. And that's why you're going to be given surgical masks. Wear them when-ever you're in contact with people. Also wear the protective gloves we give you. Death from untreated pneumonic plague is one to three days. FOR YOU

TOO! So, it's imperative that we treat victims as soon as possible.

"The treatment for plague is with antibiotics such as tetracycline and streptomycin, and is begun immediately upon discovery of the infection. All folks associated with . . . or in any contact with the patient . . . will have to be found and evaluated and probably treated. Remember this, if we can get treatment to the patient early, less than 5% will die, and if we don't, with what I think we have, you can expect 95% to die.

"We have a vaccine against plague and we will inoculate everyone in this room as soon as we break up. BUT, and this is a big but, no pun intended, we have no data on the effectiveness and safety of using the drug on persons less than 18 or older than 60. It is our intention to treat the entire community, the entire island, with both the vaccine and tetracycline therapy, if at all possible. Doctor Savage would you like to address what we're going to do about the under 18 and over 60 problem?"

I could see Doctor Joan Savage sitting on the front row, her face hidden from the audience, glaring at Doctor Allen. Hell no. She didn't want to address that subject. He'd stuck it to her. She was angry and caught off guard. Slowly the muscles in her face relaxed and she stood up and faced the crowd.

"Like Doctor Allen said, we don't have much data on seniors using the vaccine, but I'm going to authorize vaccine for everyone in this room who is over 60, with one exception. If you know you have a deficient immune system, such as from AIDS, or from a transplanted kidney or liver, please see me. As far as children go, I'll have to check with Atlanta, but I expect that we'll be able to inoculate down to six years of age or so. We just don't know how immature immune systems will hold up to the vaccine. Others over 60, we'll let you know."

Doctor Allen leaned over and whispered to Doctor Savage, "Thanks Doc, we rural hicks don't have enough malpractice insurance to handle all that."

Chapter 8

𝕴t was nearly one o'clock in the morning when I got home. As I started up the steps to the deck, I was met by good old Amos, my golden retriever, faithful companion and the youngest member of the Hale tribe. In the midst of his jumping and growling and making himself obnoxious greeting, I turned off the outside lights and went inside. My left arm was sore as hell from the plague shot and Amos' antics were beginning to piss me off. I probably hurt his feelings when I reminded him of his parentage and who he was the son of, and my tone of voice quickly put a damper on his parade.

I went to the bar and poured a generous Johnnie Walker on ice and sat in my big leather lounge chair and flipped up the footrest. I was tired, I felt half sick and I was worried to death about what was happening on the island. As I was reaching for the remote control for our satellite TV, I heard the bedroom door open and I was joined by Jo Anne dressed in blue silk pajamas and a matching robe. Since Jo Anne wakes up easily, her appearance was no surprise. "Tough evening?" she asked.

"Yeah . . . and before I forget, you need to get a plague shot tomorrow. Get to the Civic Center before seven o'clock and they'll take you right in."

"Before seven in the morning?"

"Yes."

"Will it hurt?"

"Yes, but not at first. The pain kind of starts out slow and builds over time."

"Does it work?"

"I sure hope so, because if it doesn't, there's liable to be dead people stacked around here like cord wood."

"Oh, that's a great thought to be left with just before going to bed. Is it going to be bad?"

"We sure hope not and we're taking all kinds of precautions. The first boy, Kerry, died. His two friends are in bad shape and there's a road block on the island. No one can come or leave. We're quarantined."

"But what about the storm?"

"What about it?"

"I taped a blurb from The Weather Channel for you. They say it's very bad. The winds are 98, or so, miles an hour and very rough seas. It's come north a little, and if it stays on the course it's on, it'll miss us and either go out to sea or hit up in New England somewhere. But there's a catch. A big low is over the midwest and it's moving toward the east coast. That could change everything. According to the Miami Hurricane Center the low would draw the storm toward us."

"I don't wish bad luck on anyone, but better there than here," I said after taking a long swig from my glass.

Jo Anne rubbed her nose and asked, "Why does that pull a storm toward us? Does a high push it away?"

"Sit down and I'll try to explain it to you. Do you understand what causes wind?"

Jo Anne curled up on the sofa and smiled at me. "I guess so. It's over there and it needs to get over here, so it moves"

I laughed. Perhaps the first laugh I'd had in hours. "You know, Babe, that isn't far from right. Wind is caused by air moving from a higher pressure area to a lower pressure area. The areas can be big or small and the greater the size and pressure difference the greater the wind velocity. The wind stops when it all equalizes out. Remember when hurricane Bob came through a few years back and tore off our roof shingles? And I tried to open the door and couldn't?"

"I remember you finally got the door part way open and the pressure was strong and made a loud noise."

"Right. Well, there was pressure in the house greater than outside, and when I cracked the door it caused a wind from inside the house to the outside. A very short wind, to be sure, for it only traveled about a foot or so. But as you remember, a very strong wind."

"And that's all there is to it?"

"Yes, and you know, I'll never get used to calling hurricanes Bob, or Robert, or Fred, or Dick, or Roy or Anfernee. Next thing you know, some jerk will change those named after men to himmicanes and then . . . what's the feminine for jerk, anyway?"

Jo Anne hugged a throw pillow and grinned and bit her lower lip. "I don't think there is any. I think Webster reserved that just for men."

"Oh, you do, huh? Well, then'll come personnicanes . . . and then . . ."

"Candy canes?" She asked obviously pleased with

herself.

"Good try, but I don't think so. How far away is the storm?"

"I don't remember exactly, but about a thousand miles or so."

"And the winds were what?"

"98 to 100. Do you want to hear the tape?"

"Yeah, thanks, but not right now."

"Do you want to talk?"

"Sure."

"Okay. Did you go to the house where the guys got sick?"

"Yes. Went with Sergeant Lynch and Doctor Allen and the new girl deputy . . . ah, Wanda Bowman."

"I'm sure she wouldn't want to be called a girl. Does she have short blond hair and wear sunglasses all the time?"

"No. Short dark hair, about 5-10, looks strong. Smiles a lot. I like her, but I don't think Sergeant Lynch does. She's a take charge type and you know how Hatteras men are."

"Not all of them."

"No, not all of them, but a lot. Which reminds me, do you know the requirements that a bride must meet before she can get married on this island?"

Jo Anne gave me a sly look. No, is it some

dirty joke?"

"Not at all. I got this from a native islander."

"And that makes it fact?"

"I guess as close as you're goin' to get."

"Okay. What are these hard and fast wifely requirements?"

"She should be a high school grad, have a good steady job, and all her teeth."

"I don't get it. What's the deal with her teeth?"

"It's like a horse, Babe. Good teeth, good health. Remember the movie *Roots*? Hell, they used to always check a slave's teeth before they bought one. Good teeth, good health. Dental care is expensive."

The look on her face relayed that she refused to let it go.

"You know, I'm becoming annoyed. So tell me about the house."

"Well, you know the house, where it is. It's the one with the blue roof. Has its name on a sign hanging out front . . . ah, *Sand Crab* or *Sand Fiddler* or Sand *Something*, I really don't remember. When we got there, the cottage was open, that is not locked and a lot of lights were on. We all put on rubber gloves and surgical masks. The place was a bit of a wreck with a dirty kitchen and clothes lying around. It has four bedrooms, so each fellow had his own. All were about the same with open suitcases and unmade beds and all. About what you'd expect from three young men on vacation.

"The first thing different that we all noticed was a strange sweet smell. Not very strong, but definitely different. The house had been closed up for a day or so. We all tried to place the smell and couldn't, then Wanda called it out. Hashish. It's a drug that's made from the leaves and stalks of hemp. Usually smoked in a pipe for the narcotic effect. A lot of it in the Middle East."

"I've never heard of it. Do you mean like marijuana?"

"I guess the effect is about the same, but where marijuana is chopped leaves and seeds and stalks, the hashish I've seen has always been in brick form about the size of a big flat candy bar. They must cook it or bake it or do something to it and pour it into molds. I'm told that in the U.S., one usually carves off a little from the brick and fills a pipe and smokes it. I think in the Middle East they use water pipes, kinda like you see in the movies."

"How do you know this?"

"When I was in the Navy, we had drug problems on the ships and especially after a visit to a port in Lebanon or Egypt or Morocco or Turkey. And Cyprus. Anyway, hashish does have a distinctive smell. In the kitchen we found a bar of hashish, about the size of a female Hershey Bar. Part of it was missing and with it were two pipes that looked and smelled like they'd been used recently."

"Can you get plague from hashish?" Jo Anne asked.

"No. According to Doctor Allen, bacteria won't live on or in a dry source. In the cottage, we found no evidence of rats or mice or bugs of any kind. It was too dark to check much outside. We found a trip ticket from Island Pest Control, so they do the spraying and as best we could tell, it's effective. There was absolutely nothing out of the ordinary. Well, except for a leather valise that seemed to have Egyptian artifacts in it, some scrolls and some small pieces of pottery. And on the counter in the kitchen, we found an urn that Doctor Allen became very interested in. At first he thought it was a canopic jar. It seems that they were used to store the soft organs when an Egyptian was embalmed. I guess those jars kind of looked like what we found, but should have been larger. Seems ours was too small to be a canopic jar, but Doc Allen still thought it might be some kind of burial urn because it had a wax plug. It was about eight inches tall and maybe two or three inches in diameter . . . tan with some pictures or perhaps hieroglyphs painted on it. Looked like a vase. Had some kind of a dark colored wax plug that looked to have been recently opened and then replugged."

"I didn't know Doctor Allen was so knowledgeable about Egypt," Jo Anne said. "How did that happen?"

"You know, I asked him that, and it seems that he took several Egyptian archaeological courses in college as part of a minor degree in anthropology. Well, anyway, Doctor Allen pulled the plug out and the urn had seeds in it. He said the seeds looked like wheat and he should know because he was raised on a farm. He replugged the jar and took it along to his lab to check it out. Which reminds me, just before I came home, Doc told me that he had spoken to Keith, one of the sick men from New Jersey, and Keith told him that Friday night they had smoked hashish and he remembers that Kerry opened the Egyptian jar and found the seeds. They had laughed about how the seeds might be marijuana and Kerry smelled the seeds and then wet his finger, lifted some of the seeds and then put some in his mouth. He said they tasted all right and then he put some seeds in a pipe with some hashish and smoked it. Keith said Kerry passed the pipe around, but none of them much liked the mixture so they dumped it out down the drain to the septic."

"Where did the Egyptian artifacts come from? I

mean you don't just own those."

"That's an interesting story in itself. According to one of the sick, Keith Meyers . . . I think his name's Meyers, Kerry's father is a lawyer and he collects Middle Eastern artifacts. It seems that he was recently in Egypt and bought some things. He probably smuggled them back into the U.S. According to the boys, he was going to take these items to a friend in Connecticut who is an expert and also collects with him . . . but the boys brought his utility vehicle to Hatteras, and he had already put the bag of artifacts in the vehicle and the boys unknowingly unloaded them when they unloaded after arriving at the cottage. Mister Kerry called Friday night and raised hell about them having the bag. They got curious about what was in the bag and went through it after Mister Kerry called and eventually they used a pocket knife and opened the urn. Doctor Allen's going to call an Egyptian expert at East Carolina University in the morning and check out what we found. But since bacteria can't live in or on dry seeds or in any dry environment, and the jar was definitely dry for a very long time, I don't think we have much there."

Jo Anne thought for a minute and then got up and came over and finished my drink. She stood in front of me chewing on the ice and finally said,

"You know, Fred, I wonder if bacteria can live in wax. Was the plug really big like is used when putting up jams and jellies? Is wax dry? I guess so. Let's go to bed."

I sat stunned. Maybe it could. Was she onto something?

Chapter 9

I awoke at six-fifteen Wednesday morning to a ringing telephone. Jo Anne was already up and I knew it was six-fifteen because my Big Ben wind-up alarm on the bedside table said so. I knocked my glasses onto the floor reaching for the phone and grunted good morning to whoever was calling.

"Fred, it's Tom Allen." He sounded very excited. "The reason I'm calling is I can't locate the Sheriff right off and I only have a few minutes before I'm busy as hell. Matt made you the liaison between the Medical Center and what he called Public Safety, so I'm going to unload on you what I've learned so far and you can pass it on."

"Go for it," I mumbled and tried to clear my head.

"I've found the source of the plague bacteria. After I left you and Matt last night, I returned to the Medical Center and worked most of the night in the lab on the Egyptian urn we found. I added a little moisture, and I discovered some live bacteria on the top seeds that I believe came from the beeswax stopper in the jar. The stopper was loaded with live bacteria that seemed to be in a semi-hibernated state or at least their metabolism had slowed down almost as though they had been frozen. The moisture in the air and the moisture I added to cuttings from the bottom of the beeswax plug brought forth vigorous plague bacteria who I suspect were looking for something to eat. Most bacteria feed on dead organisms and others obtain their food from living organisms. Some bacteria have simple food requirements, and can live on sunlight. Some make food from carbon dioxide as plants do. Some feed on nitrogen. Chemosynthetic bacteria obtain energy by breaking down various chemical substances such as crude oil, detergents, paint, paper, and pesticides. We use these bacteria to clean up spills. But, like man, most bacteria require oxygen in one form or another to live. Yet, other bacteria can live without oxygen. Bacteria may be only one cell, but as you can see, they're very complicated.

"Plague bacteria look unique for they resemble a closed safety pin and are called vibrio bacteria because they are bent-rod shaped. Round bacteria are called cocci, rod-shaped bacteria are called bacilli and spiral shaped are called spirilla bacteria. We have vibrio and they are about 1/2500 of an inch long. And you know bacteria are everywhere. Some live in the soil, some are carried aloft and have been found alive at 90,000 feet and others have been found at the bottom of the ocean in 35,000 feet of water. Anything that comes in contact with the air picks up bacteria, and they grow and reproduce if there is enough food available.

"Vibrio bacteria are what I found and I had a perfect match with swabs taken from Kerry. But, careful comparison between the live bacteria and the pictures I had of plague critters showed a small difference. I called CDC, Atlanta, and they were first surprised that I had found live bacteria in the jar and second, that my bacteria were of a little different form or looked a little different from what I'd expected. It baffled us to say the least. We definitely have the plague bacteria, but do we have some oddball strain? There's the rub. Are you getting all this?"

"I'm trying."

"Are you taking notes?"

"Yes," I lied. "So what you're saying is that young Kerry caught the plague from opening the jar and smoking the seeds and the others caught it the same way."

"No. We don't believe that's true. Not from the smoking of the seeds but from the tasting of the seeds. When he broke the seal, which may have been there for one hell of a long time, and exposed the plug to the air, it aroused the bacteria and his wetting his finger and tasting the seeds put the bacteria into his mouth where the warmth and wetness took over and provided food and the bacteria reproduced and spread like wildfire. Bacteria reproduce at an astounding rate. With enough food supply, they can double their number every 11 minutes. That would be one billion after six hours and with unlimited food supply they could reproduce one billion tons after 24 hours. Of course, it would be impossible to supply enough food to keep the bacteria multiplying at the maximum rate for 24 hours, but I think you get the idea."

I said, "So, one dies because the bacteria are on a feeding and reproduction frenzy in him, and essentially the blood stream becomes clogged with bacteria and bacteria crap. Is that right?"

"More or less. The other two caught the plague from Kerry. So we have the source. That's a big start. I informed CDC and they're sending two plague experts here right away and they should arrive on CDC's plane this morning. Doctor Joan Savage, the CDC gal, will meet them and set them up. She's using one of my cars."

"Where is everyone staying?" I interrupted.

"The Sea Gull Motel."

"Okay, that's good."

"Let me get on with this, Fred. I've already talked with Professor Grace Holland at East Carolina University. She's the Egyptian expert I know from school. I remembered that she was one of those kooks that get up at four in the morning and writes and studies. She still is and I got her on the telephone early this morning."

"What the hell time do you call this?"

"I call it NOW . . . She was very helpful. Listen to this! I described the urn or jar and at first she wasn't sure, then I more carefully went over the pictures and she zeroed right in on what we had. A series of circles and crosses or x's, rather like tick-tack-toe showed her that our jar was from the Byzantine or Coptic period."

"Wonderful, what does that mean?"

"The Coptic period was from 30 BC to 600 AD. For your information, Mister Hale, in 30 BC the Romans conquered Egypt in the battle at Actium where the Roman General Octavian defeated Anthony and Cleopatra, just like in the movies. After that, Egypt became a Roman Province like Israel was when Christ was born. In 500, though the pyramids had already been built, and there wasn't as much mummification going on as in the old days, many still held the old beliefs about passing into the afterworld. So, one needed to be embalmed and buried with a few useful things, and that usually included grain seed of one kind or another, so in the after life he could feed himself if it came to that. For this, the family used jars filled with seed and sealed with beeswax. Professor Holland told me that jars of seeds more than 3000 years old have been found and germinated in our time."

"Do I need to know all this, Doc?"

"Yes you do! This history is important to understanding what we're dealing with. For thousands of years Egyptian Pharaohs, as well as other Egyptian Rulers or Kings and wealthy private persons, were embalmed and buried with treasure and everyday items. Embalmers removed the soft organs like the lungs, stomach, liver and kidneys and gave the body a 70-day lye bath. A prayer was said over the body by a priest. I even wrote it down. Listen to this. *'I have come to be your protection. I embrace your body. My arms are upon you. I am filling your body with salves and all the rich minerals of the Divine Kingdom. In their stead, may the excised parts of your flesh and your clothing remain pure into all eternity.'* How's that grab you?"

"Why did you bother writing it down?"

"Because it's . . . it's important."

"Okay."

"After the praying the organs were placed in containers called canopic jars and the jars were sealed with beeswax and a carved head fitted onto them. The jars were made from stone, wood and clay, and the jar heads, no pun on the Marines intended, were carved heads of the sons of Horus, the ancient Egyptian god of the sun, who had a head of a hawk. In case you were wondering . . ."

"I wasn't wondering."

"The term canopic jar has nothing to do with the period we're talking about that's called the Coptic period that ended in 600 AD when the Arabs completed their conquering of Egypt and the Egyptians all became Islamic or were beheaded. Not surprisingly, most converted and Islam still dominates Egyptian society today.

"So, Fred, we have a jar from around 500 AD sealed with beeswax but had no carved head. That also dates it as much later than the pyramids. Now, let's talk about the beeswax. It's obtained from honeycombs of bees in the hive . . ."

"I knew that. Are you going to give me the history of beeswax?"

Just then Jo Anne walked into the bedroom with a steaming cup of coffee. Boy, did I need that. I smiled and said, "Thanks Babe, I appreciate it."

Doctor Allen asked, "Are you talking to me?"

"No, I . . . forget it. Go ahead, professor."

"Listen carefully. I'm very excited about this."

"I can tell."

"After eating large quantities of honey, bees form a waxy substance on their bodies and from this wax the bees make the honeycomb with its many cells for storing bee eggs and more honey. To get the wax, one takes the honeycomb and places it in boiling water and the wax rises to the surface where it is dipped off. Now the wax is melted again and the impurities are filtered off. For the burial jars, something was added to the wax and we don't know just what it was, but it turns the wax a dark red-yellow and gives it a nice consistency rather like taffy candy before it's cooled. The wax is stored, and when needed, it's heated again and poured into the tops of the jars to seal them.

"Now, I'll tell you what I think is the key to all this and the reason for the history lesson. Some bacteria form structures called bacterial spores. These spores are specialized cells and are among the most resistant forms of life known. Some can survive boiling water or worse and when given a food supply the spores can develop into ordinary bacterial cells of one kind or another. I think that this plague bacteria developed spores that survived in a slow or reduced state on something in the beeswax . . . and the addition of moisture awakened them, and the addition of food started a reproduction chain that eventually became a reconfigure of the spore cells to the original bacteria cells that were very aggressive plague bacteria from 548 AD, the worst and most aggressive plague in history . . . and."

"Wait a minute! So, what you're saying is that somehow the plague bacteria got into the beeswax and stayed alive in some form for over 1500 years and young Kerry popped the top and released a very bad genie. Have I got that right?"

"It's worse than that. As I said, in 548 AD the worst plague epidemic of all time swept out of Egypt and killed at least 100 million people. I spoke about it the other night at the Civic Center. Remember?"

"Yes, I do."

"Well, we may have that strain of plague here, because the timing is right. Dead right."

"Tom, has anyone talked to Mister Kerry about this?"

"No, he doesn't even know his son's dead. CDC is keeping a tight lid on."

"What if he has more of these jars or somebody does? Shoot, that's worse, or at least more scary than anything old Saddam Hussein of Iraq could do with his stores of chemical and biological warfare agents, and we're about to bomb that sonuvabitch back to the Stone Age. What Kerry did could really be worse."

"You're right and I'll get little Miss CDC on it right away if they haven't already. The CDC folks are really good, Fred, pretty damn good. It's just that Savage is a bit of a pain in the ass."

"Tom, maybe she's supposed to be."

"Could be and if that's so, she's a talented actress, cause she's got us all believing she's a horse's ass."

"Is that it?"

"No, I got more bad news. The cottage where the boys stayed could be a real problem. They poured some of this down the drain. In fact, I was told that Kerry opened the jar in the sink with a knife. The septic system of that cottage could be greatly contaminated and getting worse. Cordon it off and keep everyone away from it. We may have to burn it down and sterilize the septic system somehow. So, you'll take care of that, right?"

"Yes. Don't worry about it."

"Lastly, our vaccine program swings into full effort this morning and there's no way we can do this and not have it get out that we have a serious problem here. I'm afraid it's going to have to be on the radio and TV and in the papers to ensure we get everybody. But I can't worry about that. I understand that along with preparing for a possible hurricane the Emergency Operations folks on the island have the immunizations on their plate, too. Willie Foster's wife, Linda, will honcho it. Give her whatever help she needs from Public Safety. And another P.S., the two sick men don't seem to be responding to my drug therapy. We're using streptomycin and I'm not getting the blood readings I should. Today, I'll do more antibiotic sensitivity tests. I've told CDC."

"Do you mean that the antibiotics aren't working? WHAT ABOUT OUR GODDAMN SHOTS!!"

Tom was quiet, maybe thinking, maybe not. He dropped his voice. "I don't know, don't say anything to anyone about that, yet. I just don't know." His excitement was gone and in a whisper he said, "I'm working on it, Fred, but I just don't know."

Chapter 10

After talking with Doctor Allen, I turned on The Weather Channel and checked the progress of Hurricane Dixie. Its 0200 position was still more than one thousand miles from Hatteras, heading northwest on a course of 310 degrees at 18 miles per hour. Winds were at 98 miles per hour and the present course would make a landfall near Trenton, New Jersey. That was a relief. Better them than us. The last thing we needed right now was a hurricane.

I left the house at seven o'clock and found Sheriff Mathews at the Hatteras Sheriff's Office. I filled him in on what Doctor Allen told me, but left out the part about the problem with killing the bacteria. What with the Virginian-Pilot carrying the story of Hatteras Island "shut down tight," and the problems of maintaining the quarantine, and all the calls the Sheriff's Office was receiving in Hatteras as well as Manteo about the plague and the hurricane, he had enough things to worry about right now.

I left Matt at eight o'clock and met Tim Midgett for breakfast at Gary's Restaurant. Tim and his brother run a large real estate and development company on the island and the time had come to take some serious action and I needed his help.

Over breakfast, Tim, a tall handsome chap with dark hair, and I discussed what would be required for the County to take over the Sandy Bay Inn bed and breakfast and convert it to our first quarantine "hospital" site. It was near the Medical Center and its use made good sense. The Ramada Inn near Hatteras Landing would be our second hospital, if needed later. Tim said he would contact the folks who owned the Sandy Bay Inn and he could take care of the Ramada Inn as well, moving people out or doing whatever was necessary to make it ready.

I then brought up the problem of bodies. He seemed a little shocked that we were discussing bodies, but I allowed how it could become a problem.

"Do you have any bodies, now?" He asked.

"Yes, one. It's contaminated, but in a body bag. There could be a lot more. I think we should freeze them. How about a fishhouse with a big freezer?"

"Is it the first guy who caught the plague?"

"Yes."

"Wouldn't bodies contaminate the fishhouse?"

"Yes, they might."

"No one's going to want to let you do that, Fred."

"Oh, I'm sure you're right . . . but we have to do something, and if you can come up with something else, we'll sure listen. How about giving it some thought and kicking it around at the office?"

"Okay. How many bodies are we talking about?"

I stared at him for a second and for the first time I really focused on the possible death numbers and a chill ran through me. I picked up my coffee cup and my hand was shaking. Tim noticed and I set the cup down.

"What do you know that I don't?" he asked.

"What we have here is dangerous as hell. Have you had your plague shot, yet?"

"Yes, and it hurts."

"Make damn sure everyone you know gets one."

"Enough said. I'll be in touch. You buying?"

When I arrived back at the Sheriff's office, I

received a shock. Seven more people had been admitted to the Medical Center with plague symptoms. Two were the EMS paramedics who took the call for Kerry Monday night. One was the mother of a nursing baby along with the baby who had a temperature of 105 degrees and the other three were folks who had visited the Food Lion on Monday and had obviously come in contact with young Kerry. None had been inoculated and the doctors didn't give the baby, little Beth Comstock, any chance whatsoever.

In the midst of our planning and answering phones, we learned that Kerry's companions, Keith Meyers and John Bestul, had both passed away. Meyers at 8:30 A.M. and Bestul at 9:15. It was up to us to make the notifications and we did.

Tim Midgett called in the early afternoon to inform us that he had worked out a deal between Ezra Pound, who owned a fishhouse with a big freezer on Muddy Creek, and the County. The County could lease the fishhouse, starting today, for an indefinite period, providing the County restore or replace it at the end of the lease. Tim gave me the figure and it made sense. We were now able to warehouse our dead. Happy thought, right?

Doctor Allen called the Sheriff's Office at three o'clock and informed us that the two disease

detectives from CDC had arrived and were here to
back up Doctor Savage. They were from the CDC's
Epidemic Intelligence Service and with three doctors
now on site it was evident that CDC was taking
this plague outbreak very seriously. There would be
a meeting at 4:00 at the Medical Center with CDC
and the local doctors and they wanted a rep from
Public Safety. That would be me. I asked if it
wasn't a little hazardous to hold meetings there and
was informed that those with plague symptoms were
being sent directly to the Ramada Inn where Family
Nurse Practitioner Carey LeSieur was in charge
assisted by Doctor Hardy's RN wife, Elizabeth.
Those arriving at the Medical Center near death
were taken directly to the Sandy Bay Inn where RN
Betty Cosen was in charge of a hospice and was
assisted by women from the Village's Methodist
Church.

Four o'clock found me at the Medical Center in
the kitchen sitting around a large table with Doctor
Porter Hardy, our local senior doctor, Doctor Tom
Allen, his partner, sitting with arms crossed over his
chest and looking pissed he was there, along with
Doctor Joan Savage and Doctors Bill Hedgepath and
Ira "Bideus" Havensum, an African-American, the
last three from CDC.

Doctor Havensum was small, less than five two,

maybe 110 pounds, coal black skin and corn rows in his hair, very large eyes and, we were told, a genius on the computer. Since he had arrived less than seven hours ago, he had established a modem connection to CDC and had three computers up and working. Included, were scanning machines with color video pickup, picture and text scanners, as well as one computer hooked directly to the CDC main frame that was capable of searching all the information in the CDC files on plague bacteria. CDC had taken over Doctor Hardy's office and turned it into a bio-tech nerve center.

Doctor Hedgepath, I learned, was an authority on plague and he told us that it was he who had examined our plague bacteria and noting the difference between ours and the run-of-the-mill plague critter, thought that our bacteria looked somewhat like the deadly African Ebola virus that kills 80% of its victims. If it ever became pandemic (world wide), it could kill most of the human race for presently there's no cure. None at all. It's like AIDS, you get it, you die. You go directly to jail, you do not pass go, and there's no getting out of jail free. You die. And everyone you come in contact with dies, too. And *that's the name of that tune!*

Sometimes it's better to just not know.

So what's the deal with bacteria and viruses? Well, I'm told that there's a big difference between a virus and bacteria, but I'm not so sure that I understand exactly what the difference is. I know that bacteria are one celled microorganisms that multiply by simple division and come in various forms. Some bacteria are good and some are bad, but they all feed and unload waste and there's a school of thought that believes that bacteria are plants and not animals. End of what I know about bacteria. On the other hand, I'm told that a virus is a microscopic organism that lives in the cell of another living thing. It seems that viruses are the smallest and simplest form of life and are the major causes of disease. Viruses cause disease by damaging cells and reproducing and moving on to other cells. If enough cells are damaged, the life form dies, but usually a healthy body using its immunization system fights off the virus by producing antibodies that keep the virus from reproducing and eventually all the viruses die. This happens when you catch the common cold.

My learned friends tell me that a virus is about 1/10th the size of an average bacteria and that some viruses attack bacteria cells as well as other forms of life. Viruses also have two schools of thought about whether they are living organisms or nonliving protein cells. By itself a virus is a lifeless particle that cannot reproduce. But when a virus gets inside a living cell, it becomes an active organism and can multiply hundreds of times.

Doctor Hedgepath launched into a long discourse on how the plague bacteria looks like a closed safety pin and our bacteria happens to look like a closed safety pin too, but where the generic has only a circle where the spring would be, ours has a figure eight. And it was that figure eight that Doctor Hedgepath found similar to the Ebola virus. That virus has a figure eight or complex knot at one end and its body resembles a fishhook.

So what? So the Ebola and the plague bacteria have certain things in common. So what? They sure seem different and I doubted seriously if they had started cross breeding, so I raised my hand just like I did back in grade school and asked a question.

"So, what's the significance of the figure eight, Doctor?"

Doctor Hedgepath was tall and skinny with a bald pate above short dark hair, and deep set dark eyes looking out from behind large, thick, steel rimmed, coke bottle glasses. He was wearing a short sleeved Hawaiian flower sport shirt that was both colorful and twenty years out of date. He also had a walrus mustache that covered his upper lip and upper teeth when he talked. He was very serious, all business. He cleared his throat twice and seemed to notice me for the first time.

"The significance," he said, "is that each and every time I find a germ that has this figure eight configuration, be it bacteria or virus, I find that it is deadly and aggressive. Any outbreak must be tightly controlled. The worry, always the worry, is that one of these days a deadly, aggressive germ will come into contact with our deadliest antibiotic, it will mutate, become immune, become airborne and begin spreading throughout the animal kingdom. If all that happens, and we can't quickly come up with an effective antibiotic, then the human race could perish."

"In fact without control, AIDS could do that, right?" I asked.

"Absolutely."

Well, there you go. That answers that. A little strong? Maybe. But definitely scary, so I asked, "If an outbreak like that is all that serious, then why hasn't it happened before? Before we had antibiotics."

"It has happened before. Millions of years ago the dinosaurs became extinct. We're not really sure why, but it happened. Other life forms have become extinct. We're not even certain how old the warm blooded animal kingdom is. There's also a school of thought that if the dinosaurs hadn't died off perhaps mankind would never have evolved."

"So, you're really serious that mankind could be destroyed?"

"I certainly am. And if not destroyed, certainly pushed back to the Bronze Age. If eighty percent of the world's population died, and it occurred evenly across every nation, everything as we know it would stop. Nothing would work. And remember, most if not all the animals would die too. If, on the other hand, one large country came through it with little or no harm, then we would see colonization similar to what occurred in the 1500's through the 1800's. People left Europe and settled around the world. It would occur again. An alarming setback for our species."

Doctor Hardy interrupted. "I'd like to revisit where we are. One, we have an outbreak of the plague. Two, we know it came from an artifact brought from Egypt to the U.S. Three, we believe that the bacteria is from 500 AD and it could be the deadly form that swept the known world killing hundreds of millions of people. Four, the burial jar in which we found the bacteria alive, but in a rather dormant stage, is the only one that was brought back by Mister Kerry from Egypt. Five, three people have already died from this outbreak, and we presently have seven others who have come forward with the symptoms and are under treatment. Six, two paramedics have caught the bug even though they were immunized, but probably after the fact. Seven, immunization and antibiotic treatment is not working for those infected. It isn't even slowing down the infection, let alone killing it. Eight, all the cases seem to be from exposure to Kerry; five at the Food Lion on Monday when Kerry was ill and strolled around looking for medicine. Nine, there have been no reports to CDC from medical facilities anywhere else in the country about plague symptoms showing up in patients, so perhaps the epidemic is isolated but it's still too early to tell. And ten, thus far, no one infected has survived. Does that about cover it?"

Doctor Joan Savage quickly turned to Doctor Hardy. "There have only been three deaths," she said, "hardly enough to say that this epidemic will have no survivors. Hardly enough to say that infection means death."

The African-American, Doctor Bideus Havensum, stared at Doctor Joan Savage. He had his hands folded in front of him on the table and he shook his head and wet his lips. Softly he said, "You know, Joan, I don't know where you were raised, but where I come from we'd reckon this bacteria is batting 1000. He's putting along at 100 per cent. Every hit's a home run. His glass is full to the top and right now we have no way to stop him. Is that a fairly accurate assessment, Porter?"

"I'd say so, Bideus. And I'd just like to add that we're sure in no position to accept that old familiar axiom, *SHIT HAPPENS.*"

"Amen, brother. Amen."

Chapter 11

Sylvia knew that she had been on the bed two days, so through a throbbing headache, her body on fire from fever and then chills and then fever, she reasoned that it was Wednesday afternoon. She was still nude and tied to the bed face down, in spread eagle fashion, but the mouth tape was off and had been for some time. She could smell something cooking but she wasn't hungry and the idea of food made her stomach churn. Water. She wanted water. She was thirsty and she called out in a whisper voice but it was weak and raspy. He did not respond.

She tried to look around to see if Jack was in the room but she was so weak that she could barely move her head from side to side. The effort was draining. He seemed to be gone. He must be cooking she thought and passed out.

She woke with her face being slapped. Jack was close and talking to her. She became aware of the strong smell of shit. She started crying and her breath came in gasps.

"Well, now you've done it, Karen. You shit in the bed. Karen would never do that. Sylvia would do that, never Karen. Karen is special and dainty and clean and you're a pig. Do you expect me to clean you up? My God, I should have taken my trophy before this happened. But you see . . . I've been busy and this is a very big house and requires much of my time. I like to cook and the kitchen is perfect and thanks to you and hubby . . . did you tell me his name, Sylvia? I don't remember if you did but there's plenty of good healthy food and beer and even some very smooth scotch.

"You look like you're burning up with fever, Sylvia. Oh, I hope the fever doesn't darken your skin, or tarnish your beauty. That would be very unfortunate. For you see Karen, I'm a collector. In fact I recently added to my collection. I've been keeping it frozen in your big freezer and am now about to condition it, but first I've decided to add your trophy, so I can do both heads at the same time. Yes, you heard right, Sylvia. I collect heads much like big game hunters. But there is a difference. I don't mount them, I just save the skin and hair, and I soften the skin until it's softer than an unborn calf hide . . . then you join my harem and I keep you in a box until your time comes to please me. Let me show you what I have already."

Sylvia's head was turned out into the room and her eyes were filled with tears. She had heard what Jack had said, but none of it seemed to matter. She doubted that he would cut her head off, that was insane. He just wanted sex. She'd give that to him and he'd go away.

She felt weaker and began coughing. A huge volume of phlegm rose through her throat and settled in her mouth. She spit it out and coughed again. Now her nose was running and she was gasping for breath. She was racked with coughing and more phlegm rose and was spit out onto the pillow. She was suddenly aware that he was standing over her.

"What the hell have you done, now? I leave you for a few minutes and what? You cough and spit blood all over the pillow? You slut! I'm telling you right now, Sylvia, if I had someone else, I wouldn't even bother with you. This is the way I'm going to remember you? All covered with feces and vomit and stench? No! I'll clean you up once, but if it happens again . . . well, by God that's it. Now look over here. I want you to meet your sisters. First, in this towel is Sharlee."

A black woman's head suddenly appeared before her eyes. The black face seemed to be peering out from the towel. There was frost on the skin and the black hair was long and straight and not Negroid at all. One dark eye was open and the other was half shut, but both were flat and empty and dead.

In that moment Sylvia knew she was going to die and the chills struck again and she shivered uncontrollably. He would definitely take her head and do something with it. She shut her eyes and fear sent her heart into a tailspin and it bottomed.

Suddenly, she was calm. She had never felt so sick. Her head throbbed. Black came and then disappeared. Came again and then faded to white and then to color. She wondered what was wrong with her. She wondered how many heads he had, and then she coughed and coughed, and far away, very faintly, she thought she heard the door bell ring. She opened her eyes. It rang again! Yes, it was the door bell. For just a second Sylvia's heart soared. A glimmer of hope raced through her body. Then, something struck her neck and she lost all feeling. Bright lights flashed in her brain and then slowly, slowly, faded to black.

As she pulled into the driveway of her 41st stop of the day, a huge three story ocean front rental, in the high rent district of *Hatteras by the Sea,* Sandy Garrett, Registered Nurse, Hatteras Medical Center, pushed up the left sleeve of her white lab coat and checked her small gold wristwatch. It was one-fifty and she had missed lunch and her stomach was growling. She had been systematically covering Hatteras Village since seven o'clock this morning inoculating people against the plague in their homes and rental cottages.

A lot of folks were afraid to leave their houses for fear of catching the plague and the inoculation stations set up all over the island had drawn far fewer people than expected. So, Doctor Hardy had commenced Phase Two – an island wide house-to-house check to ensure that all the inhabitants were inoculated, sickness was reported, and everyone fully understood the quarantine and the seriousness of the matter.

Sandy was responsible for Hatteras Village and its eight hundred or so locals and an estimated fewer than one hundred visitors, this being so late in September and past the tourist season. She noticed two cars under the house one green and one black and she pulled her red Honda up behind the expensive looking black utility vehicle and parked.

Grabbing her doctor's bag from the seat, she opened her door and paused to admire the new Lincoln Navigator in front of her. "It must be nice," she muttered aloud and shut her car door and headed up the steps that led to the cottage's front door one story above. On the porch she looked to her right and counted only two more houses to canvass in this section of the village. She rang the door bell.

Sandy waited a few seconds and rang the bell again. There has to be someone here, she thought, what with all the cars below. She set her bag on the deck and knocked hard on the door and waited.

Inside, Jack Capisano, peered out a front window and studied the tall, attractive, blonde, pony tailed, woman in a doctor's coat. He saw the black bag at her feet and he couldn't understand why she was there. He wondered if she was psychic what with Sylvia so sick. She pounded on the door again and he decided to open it.

As the door opened, Sandy saw a big, dark haired, middle aged, ugly man before her wearing a T-shirt and jeans. He smiled and though he had sparkling white teeth, it didn't help his appearance much. Suddenly, she was enveloped by a strong repulsive body odor.

Sandy smiled. "Hello. I'm Sandy Garrett, a nurse with the Medical Center. I'm canvassing the

SOUND & FURY • 105

neighborhood to ensure that everyone has had their plague shot. Have you?"

Jack looked surprised. "What plague shot?"

"Are you aware that we have a plague outbreak here on Hatteras Island?"

"No, I'm not."

"Have you been watching television or reading the paper or listening to the radio?"

"No, not really. I've been busy."

"For the record, what's your name?"

"Ah, Jack. Jack Johnson."

"Are you renting?"

"Yes."

"From Midgett Realty?"

"Ah . . . yes, I think so."

"Mister Johnson, I noticed two cars under the house. Who else is here?"

"No one."

"No one else is staying here?" Sandy was skeptical.

"Why do you ask?"

"We have to ensure everyone gets the shots. Are you certain no one else is staying here?" Sandy smelled a love rendezvous, but she wondered who would rendezvous with this guy?

Jack studied the woman before him. He thought she was pretty, very pretty. He especially liked her

sparkling blue eyes and he thought she resembled
some movie actress. Maybe some movie about the
water. She was a mermaid. *Splash*? That was it,
Splash, but what was her name? Couldn't remember.
What an addition to his harem she would be. Yes,
he'd collect her, too. Things were looking up. Two,
no, three beautiful additions in just a few days. He
looked directly into Sandy's eyes and smiled.

"What did you ask?"

Sandy repeated, "Are there others staying in the
house?"

"Just my wife. She came in a different car. I was
on the road and we met here. A little get away
from the kids. She's sleeping right now. Should I
go get her?"

"I need to give you both a plague shot. Why
don't I give you yours, and then you can wake her
and I'll give her hers. Does she feel all right?"

"I think she's just tired. Why don't you come in
and give me mine now? What does it cost?"

"It's free, Mister Johnson, and I'm going to leave
some antibiotics for you, too. Both you and your
wife are to take four tablets a day. When did you
arrive in Hatteras?" Sandy asked as she was led up
a short flight of stairs to a great room area with a
huge kitchen. The kitchen had an aroma like
cabbage cooking with something else tossed in. She

placed her bag on the counter and opened it.

"We arrived on . . . Monday. Yes, that's right. Monday. I remember because we stopped at the Food Lion and bought groceries for the week."

"You were in the Food Lion on Monday?"

"Yes, well, my wife was. I wasn't. I didn't go in. I stayed in the car. In my car. We had two cars. She shopped."

"Pull your sleeve up and I'll give you the shot in your upper arm. Which arm?"

"My left."

"But before I do that, let me take your temperature. I'll just put this in your ear. All right?"

"Sure."

After waiting a few seconds, Sandy withdrew and checked the thermometer. "Mister Johnson, you have a slight temperature. Do you feel warm?"

"No. Can't say as I do."

"And your wife feels all right?"

As the needle plunged into his shoulder, Jack suddenly realized why he was being asked all the questions. "What does the plague do to you? In other words what are the symptoms?"

"Fever. Chills. Stomach aches. Diarrhea. Black spots under the arms and in the groin. Coughing up blood. Serious business," Sandy said as she put away her paraphernalia.

"Are people getting it who were at the Food Lion on Monday?"

"We think so."

"Are they giving it to others?"

"We're afraid that could happen."

"And if you get the shot, you're okay?"

"We hope so. It should make you immune."

"How do you get it from another person?"

"With this form we believe it'll be spread through coughing and sneezing, much like a cold."

"Kissing?"

"Of course . . . Ah, Mister Johnson, is your wife sick? If she is, you must tell me because she could be very contagious. I need to see her, now."

Jack reached back and withdrew his knife from its scabbard on the back of his belt and placed it under Sandy's chin. "Let's go see Sylvia together, Nurse Sandy. Pretty name, Sandy. Very pretty, like Karen."

Chapter 12

Can animals get the plague? Sure they can. Bites from fleas, but what about through a cough. Didn't someone say that cats could give the plague to humans by coughing on them? Would my pal Amos get the plague? Could I give him a shot? Did I need to worry about it? I'll keep him locked up. How were the islanders holding up? Where was the hurricane?

All these questions ran through my mind as I drove from the Medical Center home for dinner. I felt all right, maybe a little tired. Jo Anne was staying home and I knew we had enough supplies in the pantry and freezer so that we could hold out for days from shopping.

Our supply system onto Hatteras Island had truly

become convoluted. Trucks brought trailers of food and other supplies to the Marina at the foot of Bonner Bridge that spans Oregon Inlet and connects Bodie Island to Hatteras Island. There the trailers were left and a Dare County tractor with a fifth wheel was used to move the trailer onto the bridge where it was left heading south for pick up by another Dare County tractor that couldn't leave the island. Once on the island the trailers were hostage to the quarantine. Thus far the system was working, but it really hadn't been fully tested because folks were afraid to leave their homes for any reason, least of all to shop in the vicinity of other shoppers who might give them the plague. So, there hadn't been a run on stores. No traffic jams on Highway 12.

Island wide all restaurants and most other shops were closed. Those folks you did see out and about all wore the circular red stick-on given when you got inoculated and had printed on it *I'VE BEEN SHOT*. A little humor in the midst of this mess was welcome and this *Red Badge of Courage* quickly identified all who hoped they were safe.

Surgical masks were being worn at the Medical Center and by EMS paramedics and ambulance drivers, at the Ramada Inn Hospital and the Sandy Bay Hospice, and some were reportedly seen on other folks out and about, but thus far they weren't the rage. True panic hadn't yet set in.

The Coast Guard had stopped and arrested a total of thirteen people trying to leave the island by boat and interestingly all were wearing their "red badge." They were returned to their homes and their boats confiscated.

One van full of surfers had tried to run the road block at the Bonner Bridge but was stopped and the four young men and two women were arrested and returned to The Hatteras School gym where the "homeless" were being processed and fed.

I was happy that the populace of the island was really coming together, pulling with one oar as it were, for we are usually very tribal and rarely socialize between villages. That may seem odd to the outsider, but it's true. I don't know that there's any real reason for it. It just happens.

During dinner, Sheriff Mathews called and said he wanted me back at the office ASAP. It seems that Sandy Garrett, a nurse from the Medical Center, had disappeared.

It was after dark when I walked into the Hatteras Sheriff's Office next to the Volunteer Fire House and was met by Matt, Lieutenant Randy Howard and Jerry Wilson both deputies. I wasn't surprised to see Randy but Jerry Wilson was a different matter. He lives alone in Manteo and was off the island when the quarantine went into effect. Now he's here. How did he get here? Never mind, for we really needed him because people sure weren't rushing south.

Jerry was a ten-year veteran Detective Sergeant with the Baltimore Police Department when he lost his foot from a shotgun blast during a shootout one night. Baltimore gave him a new foot and then a kiss and a kick (a medal and disabled retirement) and he moved to the Outer Banks and joined the Dare County Sheriff's Department.

Jerry is a little guy, about thirty-six or seven, with thinning blond hair, a narrow face, thick horned rimmed glasses and has all the complexes that come to some who are height challenged. Occasionally he wears contacts, but not tonight. His wooden foot produces a slight limp but, all in all, he is greatly respected by the other deputies and Matt has confided in me that he considers Jerry to be his best investigator.

Jerry, the consummate professional, has no love for me because he thinks I'm a shoot from the hip, dangerous amateur who should get lost. We did, however, reach a compromise during our last murder investigation and now we can co-exist in the same room for more than an hour at a time.

"How the hell did you get here, Jerry?" I asked.

"I heard you men needed help, so I brought a truck loaded with supplies on down. County stuff that may be needed if Hurricane Dixie hits here. No big deal. I've had my shot."

I turned to Matt. "What do we have on Sandy Garrett?"

"Fred, we don't know. She was out today doing inoculations in the village and was supposed to be back at the Medical Center before dark. She hasn't shown up. I'm told this isn't like her. She regularly checks in and lets people know where she'll be. Last heard from about noon and getting ready to check out *Hatteras by the Sea*. We called her husband and she's not home and they haven't heard from her all day. We drove through the area but didn't see her car. There aren't a great number of cottages there, and only a few are rented, and we're about to do a house-to-house inquiry."

"Isn't it a little early to tie up resources doing that now?" Jerry asked. "Seems to me that we should patrol and try to find her car. Find the car probably find her."

Matt glared at Jerry. "Jerry, I've thought of that. I'm reading the same book you are, goddamn it, I'm not coloring in it."

Jerry's face fell. "I didn't mean to imply that you were . . ."

"Stupid? No, I didn't think you did. I have a plan, let's just do it." Matt leaned back in his chair. "Sandy Garrett is out there somewhere, with someone, probably helping someonc, and we just have to find her. I'll grant you, it isn't easy to lose a person or a car here but it certainly isn't difficult to hide. The car could be anywhere, under any house, behind some . . . something. Inside a damned garage."

"Matt, how much sleep have you had in the last two days?" I asked.

"Not a hell of a lot. When am I supposed to sleep? Between emergencies? Right now that's just a little difficult, wouldn't you say?"

"Yes, but you're no good to us or yourself if you aren't rested."

"You saying I outta go home and go to bed?"

"I'm just saying you look tired and should get some rest. We'll check out the *Hatteras by the Sea* area. Stop at the houses and see if she's been there."

"Go ahead!"

The trip turned out to be uneventful. We pulled into every driveway and checked under every house.

No red Honda. Six houses had occupants. All six households had their shots. Folks from two cottages had gone to the Civic Center to be inoculated and the other four families or groups had been inoculated by Sandy that afternoon.

Everyone had been cordial and helpful except for Mister Wissenhunt who was staying in Judge Reinhold's ocean front cottage. He and his wife wouldn't open the door so I had to talk through the closed door with him. He had said that until the plague thing was over he wasn't leaving his house and no one was coming in. Can't say as I really blame him much. He also told me that a tall blond nurse had come by about two and had given him and his wife their shots and had left before two thirty. He said he hadn't seen her car but he thought he heard it start up after she left. There was in fact a red "I've been shot" sticker on the outside of the front door. Placed there by Sandy, I was certain.

The last house at the end of the cul-de-sac had eight male surf fishermen staying in it and they had gotten shot at the Civic Center and had spent the day at the beach fishing and never saw Sandy or her little red car. They didn't return to the cottage until after five thirty so she was probably there and they missed her. Folks from two of the cottages remembered that she drove up in a red car but no one saw her leave the subdivision. It seems she came, she saw, she left. Not quite as dramatic as Caesar who came, saw and conquered, but where the hell was she?

Chapter 13

At three thirty in the morning the wind changed from southwest to northeast and the rains came. I know this because I got home at two ten and was still awake when the rain drops started hitting the skylight in my bedroom. The rain had come down hard for ten minutes or so and then had slacked off and I drifted off only to wake with a start at five-fifteen.

I swung my legs down onto the carpet and shook my head to clear it. Immediately, Amos, who sleeps on the cool tile in the master bathroom, padded out and over to the bed and stuck his head on my thigh. I slowly petted him as my eyes tried to penetrate the darkness.

A dream had awakened me. I'd had it before, in

fact many times before. A young woman clad in a flimsy white gown, chasing me. It was always the same, her breathing rapid and shallow and her nipples hard and visible through the fabric. She had no head. She had no neck either. Always an incomplete body, and the sound of breathing, and the erotic breasts.

Jack Capisano! The sonuvabitch! A man I had one time thought was my friend. A collector. A collector of human parts. Oh, not pieces parts like old Jeffery Dahmer, the Michigan cannibal. But because of Jack, I had the dream over and over.

Suddenly, I was wide awake. Jack Capisano. I really hadn't thought much about him even after the heads up from the FeeBees. What had Bev said about him? Driving a green van maybe headed our way. Not much help there. Most new vans are some shade of green. Was he on the island? Had he somehow captured Sandy and was holding her? Not likely. Would we eventually find her body somewhere out in the open, like the others?

Sandy was last seen visiting cottages and giving shots. Where the hell was her car? We'd looked just about everywhere. Where hadn't we looked? In garages. Well, there weren't many garages in Hatteras Village, but what about on the whole island? Many garages. Too many garages. Sooner or later we'd find the car. It couldn't leave. We had decided to broadcast her disappearance over the local radio station, WYND, and ask everyone to be on the lookout for her or her car. Patrols would continue looking but what else could we do?

I went out into the kitchen and was puttering around when Jo Anne arrived on scene and started making some coffee. She sensed I was more troubled than when I had arrived home and she was kind enough to let this old dog chew his own bone. She just gave me a smile and went back to bed. But not Amos. He stood by my side and watched the rain strike our big glass double doors.

At six o'clock I got the weather report and jotted down the 0200 position of Hurricane Dixie for Jo Anne to enter into her computer. The Thursday morning position was 891 miles from Hatteras on a course of northwest with winds of 98 miles per hour. Still headed for New Jersey or New York if we were lucky. The report had said though that the analysts were concerned about the pressure for it was 961 millibars and falling. That meant that the winds were bound to get stronger and the low centered over the Midwest was now slowly moving eastward and would soon influence the hurricane. Its present track would take it right over Bermuda Friday morning and that would give us a strong indication of what it was all about. One more day.

I thought about what I should do in preparation for the hurricane and decided that there really wasn't much I could do right now. I had plenty of plywood in the garage to board up if it came to that and I'd ask Jo Anne to start putting things away and be thinking about what to do if another storm hit like Emily in 1993. I resolved we'd be better prepared this time.

Bobbie Adams, our friend and neighbor and the office manager of the Medical Center, called Jo Anne as I was putting on my purple rain slicker and preparing to leave for the "office." Actually, the slicker is purple and blue and was a gift, so I wear it even though I feel and look like a stylish nerd. That's always been my luck. When everyone else has a yellow one, I end up with a purple one. By the time this SOB wears out and I buy a yellow or black one, I suppose everyone will have an international orange one. Sometimes you just can't get in step.

When Jo Anne got off the phone, she looked stricken. There were tears in her eyes.

"What's the matter, Babe?" I asked concerned.

"Katy Lee woke this morning with a high fever and sick to her stomach. She has the plague."

Katy Lee is Bobbie and Monnie Adams' college

daughter who attends East Carolina University over in Greenville.

"What the hell is she doing here? College started several weeks ago, didn't it?"

"It seems she has no classes on Mondays and was home this past weekend and Monnie backed his truck into her car on Monday evening as she was preparing to leave for school and busted the radiator. She decided to take her mother's car to school on Tuesday and all hell broke loose and then she was quarantined."

"Did she get a shot?"

"Yes, yesterday morning."

"Where's she been?"

"The weekend and Monday and Tuesday she was down at Teach's Lair Marina helping Joe with inventory. She's been home and there."

"Are Bobbie and Monnie all right?"

"Yes, and they all got their shots at the same time."

"Christ, Jo Anne, what if these goddamn shots don't work?"

After I left home, I dropped by the Medical Center and put on a surgical mask and went back to Doctor Tom Allen's lab.

I knocked and pushed the door open. He was

sitting on a stool looking into a microscope. Slowly, he looked up and turned toward me. I sat down on another stool. "How's it going, Doc?"

His eyes were pinpricks and a bead of sweat was on his brow. He looked drugged. "You shouldn't be here, Fred," he mumbled and turned back to his microscope.

"Sue me."

Still leaning over his microscope he said, "If you're staying, put on some surgical gloves. They're in the white box."

"Okay, but can you give me a minute?"

"I suppose so."

"You look like shit, what are you taking?"

"Lots of coffee. Vivarin to keep me awake. B-12."

"How about leveling with me about this plague."

"What do you want to know?"

"Give me an overview."

"Not for publication, right?"

"Between you and me, Doc."

"I'm doing antibiotic sensitivity tests and nothing is working."

"Which means?"

"Means that I can't kill the bacteria. It seems that once the bacteria takes hold we can't stop it. There's no cure."

"What about the inoculations?"

"Mostly, they seem to be working if folks weren't exposed to the bacteria before they were shot. At least so far that seems to be the case. CDC feels that it's because, given time, the vaccine makes our immune system antigens deadly to the bacteria. But we don't know why. So far we can't replicate the process in the lab. We're backing the shots up with tetracycline antibiotic chemo-prophylaxis and I . . ."

"Wait a minute, Tom. On the what?"

"You're taking four tablets a day of 500 milligrams of tetracycline. That recommendation was inferred by CDC from experience with the drug in treating plague in India. There haven't been any controlled trials that actually demonstrated the efficacy of tetracycline chemoprophylaxis in preventing plague."

"Then what the hell are we all taking it for?"

"Because we don't have anything else. Okay?"

"Katy Lee has the plague," I blurted out.

"I know. Porter told me."

"She had her shot yesterday and she was on the chemowhatsashit therapy. It didn't work."

"I know. Hopefully, she came in contact with the bacteria before her shot."

"Hopefully? What do you mean hopefully? That

means she's gonna die, right?"

"But many others wouldn't. It'd mean that the vaccine is working and maybe the drug therapy is helping."

"Are she and the paramedics the only ones who have reported in sick after having the shots?"

"Unfortunately, not . . . and the paramedics both died this morning. We now have sixty-one cases we're treating. Another death last night. A baby. The mother is sicker than hell. Probably won't make it. Another, Mrs. Thelma Marley from Avon, 81, she's not going to make it. A Mister Barton . . . no, Martin, has emphysema and a bad heart and the plague. I'm afraid he'll probably die this morning."

"What are we going to do about Katy Lee?"

"The same as I'd do for anyone. I'm trying."

"Besides the paramedics, has anybody else from Public Health or Public Safety contacted it?"

Tom didn't answer.

"Well, has anybody? What's the matter?"

"I may have it, Fred."

"Are you serious?" I said sliding from my stool and slowly moving away.

"I'm beginning to show some symptoms, but I haven't done a blood culture, yet. I was just about to when you came in. Maybe, I'm just tired and worn out . . . I don't know, I've tried about everything, streptomycin, tetracyclines, and several sulfonamides in my sensitivity tests . . . and what else. Yes, chloramphenicol."

"Yeah, but you aren't the only guy working on this."

"That's true. I have the two gents from CDC here and a tremendous source of information through them, but they don't have the bacteria in Atlanta. I have it here and it can't be taken from here, not now."

"I understand that, but what are you going to do now?"

"I've got one or two ideas. I haven't tested Bactrim. It's an antibiotic combination of trimethoprim and sulfamethoxazole. I haven't tried another antibiotic called cephalosporin either. And I haven't tried combinations of these with the others."

"And then?"

"I've asked CDC to send me any new fluoroquinolones that haven't been approved by the FDA as yet and are still undergoing clinical testing. These'll be the absolute 'drugs of last resort.' I don't have any here, we're not in the testing program, but hopefully, I'm receiving something new via CDC's plane from Atlanta. A flouroquinolone called ofloxcin is very powerful but it's never been used to fight plague. I've got some, I'll try it, might work. It might be our last shot."

"Tom, pardon me for saying so, but all of this sounds like throwing spaghetti on the wall and seeing if any of it'll stick. This is where we are? We can walk on the goddamn moon, we can miniaturize anything and we can't kill a little bacteria?"

"Welcome to science, mighty engineer. You think in absolutes. This won't fall down, this will. This won't break, this will. I have to deal in science. I have to deal in what we know. I have to try things until something works. You'd never do that. You'd never build a bridge, try it and if it didn't work, build another one and another one until you built one that didn't collapse under traffic. You'd never do that. For an engineer that doesn't make any sense. Science . . . science is different. I have to keep poisoning these critters until something kills them. When it does, then I've won. If I can't, then for now, we lose."

"You haven't got much time, my friend."

"Maybe the gods will smile."

"That sounds like voodoo, Doctor Frankenstein."

"It is voodoo. You got a better idea?"

I opened the door, winked at Doctor Tom and left.

Chapter 14

As we took off from our little one runway air field, The General Billy Mitchell, climbed, heading south, I loosened my seat belt and spoke to the pilot through the intercom. "Keep her low and slow, Don."

We were flying in an old one engine green and orange Piper Cub with rumble seat that took off at about 55 miles per hour and could keep itself airborne at as slow as 40 miles an hour with just two of us in the plane. Don Phillips owned and operated Don's Flying Service and usually took folks sightseeing around Hatteras and Ocracoke Islands. Today Dare County Sheriff's Office had hired him to squire me around to look for Sandy Garrett's red Honda.

The rain had stopped and I had come equipped with a clip-on radio and was in contact with the Sheriff's Department vehicles that were out on patrol. Two were assigned to the village and others at each village on northward through Rodanthe. Deputies Wanda Bowman and Dwayne Haskins were patrolling Hatteras Village. Bowman had the ocean side and Haskins the sound side.

We flew at 100 feet and were over *Hatteras by the Sea* almost immediately. We flew to the inlet and turned around and flew the sound side. There are a lot more trees and uncut brush than you would expect thirty miles off the North Carolina Coast. At Durant Point we turned south again and flew Highway 12 to the ferry docks. No red Honda sighted.

"Don, fly me back to *Hatteras by the Sea* and drop your right wing and fly in a tight circle over each of the cul-de-sacs, all this just doesn't make sense. That damn car has to be somewhere. We've driven every street and checked under most of the cottages. We'll do this and then head north toward Frisco."

"No problem, Fred. But what do you expect to find by doing this? We've flown over that little area twice now and found nothing. She could be anywhere from here to fifty miles north."

"She disappeared near *Hatteras by the Sea* and I'm convinced that her car is here somewhere. None of those cottages have completely closed-in garages . . . and what the hell's that?"

We were over a short cul-de-sac just past the community's private swimming pool. A deep corner lot ran from the street and sided the cul-de-sac. It hadn't been cleared and tall bushes and grass and stubby trees filled 90% of the area and blocked the view from the streets, but from the air I had seen something red.

"Don, ease over the wooded lot. There it is! I'm sure of it. A red car near the center of the lot. Completely hidden by the big bushes."

"How'd it get in there, Fred? I don't see any, yes, I do. At the end of the cul-de-sac, over the short grass, between those two trees and around the bushes . . . kiss my ass, if you'd ever find it from street level. Pretty smart, but who put it there?"

"That's the question, Don. That's the $64 question."

Sandy sat on the floor of the closet with her back against the side wall, her long legs stretched out in front of her, the locked door to her right. Her hands were taped behind her back, her ankles were taped together and her mouth was taped over with the duct tape wound around her head. She was scared, her mouth was dry, she had a terrible thirst, and she had no idea how long she had been in the closet. She knew she had slept for a while, maybe twice or three times. She just couldn't remember. At first she had tried to work her hands free but all that happened was that the tape got tighter. By moving around she had learned that the closet was empty, completely empty, not even any hangers. And the door was strong. This was not your common garden variety hollow core closet door that could be kicked open. No, this was a solid, wood paneled door with a keyed lock. She had wondered why anyone would want to lock their closets and then she thought about rental property and maybe she was in the owner's closet and it was kept locked, but now there wasn't anything in it. Maybe there was more than one owner's closet.

Sandy felt relieved that Jack Johnson hadn't harmed her as yet. She remembered how quickly he had taped her hands and mouth. And how scared she got when he pinched her nostrils together and she couldn't breathe. And he did it over and over and over until she was certain it was a game. Maybe a lesson. His control. He controlled her life with just the touch of his fingers.

Then he had her climb some stairs and they

entered a huge bedroom that stunk from feces and urine. A nude woman was on her stomach tied to the bed. Her face was turned out toward the room and her eyes and mouth were open. She was dead.

Sandy remembered looking away quickly and her focus had centered on one of the bedroom's overstuffed chairs. A black face looking out from a towel. It was a head and right then she knew. Not Mister Jack Johnson, no indeed. Jack Capistrano. My God! Jack Capistrano, the Headhunter. She had been shocked and terrified and would have screamed if she'd been able.

He had ripped the tape from her mouth and had spoken in a soft deep voice. "Sylvia is a mess, isn't she? She died easily, though. Just a blow to the back of the neck. There's a weak link there, but of course you know that being a nurse and all. She was to be my Karen . . ." He paused and smiled showing perfect teeth. "My harem Karen."

Sandy remembered licking her lips and mumbling, "You're Jack Capistrano, the Headhunter, aren't you?" He had laughed. "Not Capistrano, that's a place. Capisano's my name . . . and headhunting is my game. The Headhunter." He had laughed again and said that he liked it. He had asked who named him that? "Do you know? Was it Fred Hale? He was my friend. We used to play golf and drink beer and talk baseball." His voice rang in her ears. "I liked him but he's a lawman. Sheriff's friend. They got too close. I think they knew I killed Larry Hyatt. If they knew I was here they'd come after me. But they don't know I'm here. You do! Only you. I don't feel well, I'm taking a little nap and then I'll show you my harem. Come with me." She remembered every word as though they had just been spoken and she recalled that he had taken her out of the bedroom and into another bedroom with green carpet and had retaped her mouth, had thrown her into the closet and she had heard the keys jingle as he locked the door.

Now, she was still in the closet, she needed to go to the bathroom and he hadn't come back. He hadn't returned. Not once. And her antibiotics! She needed to take her antibiotics. She wondered if she should bang on the door. She thought not. Better to leave well enough alone.

Chapter 15

The closet door opened and Sandy awoke with a start. The sunlight blinded her and she blinked and blinked and shook her head. She was pulled roughly to her feet and the tape cut from her ankles. Her legs were weak and she wobbled back and forth fearful she would fall. She was still wearing the lab jacket.

Jack rose from the floor, his huge buck knife still in his hand. He waved it before Sandy's face. She was watching the knife and suddenly Jack came into focus. He looked terrible. His eyes were sunken with black circles and the whites were red and bloodshot. His nose was running, dropping snot, and his face was flushed, his cheeks red. Beads of sweat stood out on his forehead and he was trembling. He was wearing a long, dark blue, terry cloth bathrobe tied around his middle and with the monogram JB on the pocket. His breathing was raspy and he suddenly went into a coughing fit that bent him over. When he pulled his hand away from his face, it was full of bloody phlegm and he wiped it on his bathrobe. She knew he had the plague. She also knew it was fairly far along and he would probably die.

He straightened up to full height of more than six feet and squared his shoulders. "Sit on the bed," he whispered.

She tried to walk but couldn't make her legs move. Her shoulders ached and her arms were numb.

"Sit on the . . . BED!!" He demanded.

Sandy slowly moved her right leg and then her left and made her way across the large green carpeted room and sat on the side of the bed. Her hands were still taped behind her back and she tried to work herself into a position that wasn't uncomfortable.

"Sit still . . . I'm sick and you have to help me. I've brought your bag up here and I need to know what to take. I can't think straight. What pills do I take?"

Sandy made a sound in her throat. He stared at

her. "You need the tape off your mouth. Take it off! It's okay. Take it off but don't say anything or scream or I'll cut you, I'll cut you good."

Sandy made another noise in her throat and shrugged her shoulders.

Jack watched her. Slowly he wiped his nose with the back of his hand, his brow with his finger tips and moved to the bed. As he placed his knife behind her ear, Sandy took in a sharp breath and held it. She felt the large blade work into her hair and up alongside her head. Then, with a pull, the tape was cut and he quickly unwrapped it pulling hair and skin. She gasped and then was free to speak.

Tears flowed into her eyes. "I need some water," she rasped.

"Go get some in the bathroom."

"I can't," she whispered.

"Why not?"

"My hands are tied." Her voice had returned.

"Wait there."

Jack walked into the connecting bathroom. Sandy heard the water flowing, then he returned with a paper cup in one hand and the knife in the other. She thought he was about to collapse.

"Here. Open your mouth." He held the cup as she drank.

"I need to go to the bathroom."

"That's out of the question."

"If you want me to help you, I must go to the bathroom."

"No."

"Cut my hands free."

"No."

"Cut my hands free, NOW!"

"No!"

"Then, Jack Capisano, you're going to die. Without my hands free I can't help you. Not at all."

"No!"

"You need another shot," she lied, "some antibiotics, and you need them right away. So, untie me!"

Jack swung around and staggered to the bedroom door. He locked it and shoved one of the overstuffed chairs in front of it.

"You make one move to leave and you're dead."

"I understand. Please cut me loose."

He did.

"Leave the bathroom door open."

She did.

Doctor Tom Allen had checked his blood and though he had been fearful that he was infected with the plague bacteria he found no evidence of it in his system. With a sigh of relief he left his makeshift lab and strolled to the CDC computer clearing center that had been set up by CDC's Doctor Bideus Havensum and his cohort Doctor Bill Hedgepath. Both men were sitting behind computers. Doctor Hedgepath was scanning a thick printout, his coke bottle glasses perched on his nose and the top of his head shinning. The bottom of his thick mustache was wet from being sucked into his mouth and tongued, a nervous habit he seemed to have when reading.

Doctor Allen smiled and said, "Hello, guys, I've tried everything and I'm now stain testing combinations of all the antibiotics. It'll be about 12 to 18 hours before I know for sure, but so far, nothing seems to work on this bacteria once it starts reproducing. Until I get the clinical trial stuff, has anybody got any ideas?"

Doctor Havensum looked up but offered nothing. Doctor Hedgepath nodded his head. "I've got one," he said. "But first let me tell you about this. We just got a report from CDC that three cases of plague have been reported to them. Two on Wednesday and one today. Wednesday's were from Clinton, Pennsylvania, and Cleveland, Ohio. Today's is from Norfolk, Virginia. All three patients visited the Outer Banks last weekend and left the island either Monday evening or Tuesday morning. All three were at the Food Lion in Avon on Monday. CDC is doing an intensive follow up with the families and others these folks may have been in contact with. So my friends the bug is off the island.

"Now, about my idea. A laboratory at Kansas State University working in conjunction with Duke University Medical School has been experimenting with a new antibiotic using something called triflurpenomethoxin. They're trying to develop a shock treatment for fast acting pulmonary infections. Fast acting really means deadly. This stuff's a very toxic compound . . . in fact it's a deadly poison but the labs have discovered that when used in minute amounts and absorbed in aluminum hydroxide, and diluted with a saline solution, and then added to a quart of blood and allowed to assimilate in the blood, and as 007 used to say 'stirred not shaken,' then given to the patient through a transfusion, it seems to kill every known bacteria and promotes the cleansing of the bloodstream. But there's a big problem. It's administered by body weight and too much triflurpeno damages the immune system and the liver of the recipient. As I remember, the amount of damage done is directly dependent upon the amount of triflurpeno used. Not enough work has been done to establish just how fast and how completely the damaged organs and the immune system are restored."

"Is this in the mouse stage or has it been used on humans?"

"India. The Indians picked up on the research and I believe have had some human trials with it or something like it, but as far as I know there haven't been any human trials in the United States. I'm going to check back through CDC and see how up to speed they are on the Indian work. But even if the Indians have had a breakthrough that doesn't mean we can get permission to use it."

"I know, but that's neither here nor there. If I get hold of it, and I have people dying, and this stuff just might work, then by God, I'll use it. As the attending physician, I can make that decision. Get everything you can on it. We're grasping for straws here."

Bideus scratched his head and said, "I may be wrong, but wasn't it Sherlock Holmes who said that it's a capital mistake to theorize before one has data?"

"I'm not theorizing, Bideus, I'm planning. And Bill, when can I expect the stuff from CDC?"

"It should be on the island in a couple of hours,

Tom. You know, you don't look so good. Do you feel all right? Bideus and I can meet the plane, do the pick up and get the antibiotics back here."

"Thanks, I'd appreciate that. I'm just tired, but I need to get over to the Ramada Inn. I was just notified we have several more patients to intern. It looks like we're starting to get the snowball effect. You know, nothing's easy."

By the time Don and I landed at the Billy Mitchell Airport and I drove to *Hatteras by the Sea* and joined the flurry of police activity going on there, Sandy Garrett's red Honda had been moved to the Hatteras Court cul-de-sac and the car had been gone over carefully. I was met by Sheriff Matt, Jerry Wilson, our wooden footed detective, and Lieutenant Randy Howard who actually ran the Hatteras Island portion of the Dare County Sheriff's Department. The State Police were represented by Sergeant Mel Norrick and his sidekick Patrolman Phillip Morris. That's right, Patrolman Phillip Morris from Raleigh, North Carolina. Now, you just know there's a story there and probably a rough childhood. Nearby on the lot was a Midgett Realty "For Sale" sign with a "Call Dan Johnson" addendum.

"What's the plan?" I hurriedly asked the group. Everyone looked to Sheriff Matt. "We were just discussing that. No clues to her disappearance were found in the car and we've searched the area and there's no body. No sign of her. She could have been taken somewhere, but we don't think so. No one in the cottages saw the red car enter the bushes. Of course none of the cottages with the best and clearest view of this cul-de-sac and wooded lot are rented. But, still, I think maybe she's here in one of these cottages. I hope like hell she's here in one of these mega-dollar cottages. There aren't that many of them, so we'll split up and ask to search the ones that are occupied and search for evidence of a break-in on those that don't seem to be occupied. If anyone refuses to allow us to search, I want that reported to me at once and I'll take it from there."

Chapter 16

Sheriff Mathews and I stood leaning against the left front fender of his car, the driver's door fully open, and listening to feedback sputtering from his radios. There wasn't much to say, the search was on and sooner or later . . .

It was sooner.

"Sheriff Mathews, this is Deputy Wilson. Several of us are down here at . . . what's the number? What is it? . . . 55189. Sign on the front reads Judge and Catherine Reinhold, Fredericksburg, Virginia. There are two vans under the house, both locked. One is a black Lincoln Navigator with Virginia plates and the other is a dark green Plymouth Astor with Florida plates. We've knocked and pounded on the cottage door but received no reply. All doors are locked and we've observed no occupants through the windows on the main deck. It appears that no one is home. Over."

Matt sat in the driver's seat and picked up his microphone. "Well, Jerry, they could be fishing or sleeping."

"They couldn't be sleeping, Sheriff, not with the racket we've been making. Over."

"What was the number on the house again?"

"5-5-1-8-9."

"And what's the name of this street?"

"Lighthouse Road, West."

"I'll get right back to you, Jerry."

"You know, Matt, Capisano was reported driving a green van," I said.

"Christ! You're right. I completely forgot about him . . . well, I didn't forget about him, but I don't expect to run into him. But you're right, that's a consideration."

Matt reached over and took his cellular phone and handed it to me.

"What's this for?"

"It's so you can call information and get Judge Reinhold's telephone number in Fredericksburg and see what we can find out. In the meantime I'm going to call 911 communications and get the telephone number of that cottage . . . and since you're on my phone, I'll have Clark, he's on duty now, call and see if we can get an answer. So don't stand there, get calling."

The information operator informed me that the telephone number for Judge Reinhold was unlisted. I informed her that I was a deputy sheriff in North Carolina – she asked for our code – I gave it to her and she gave me the unlisted phone number and made the connection.

Three rings and an elderly woman's voice.

"Hello, Catherine Reinhold."

"Mrs. Reinhold, I'm Deputy Sheriff Fred Hale of the Dare County Sheriff's Department. You own an ocean front cottage in Hatteras Village in a subdivision called *Hatteras by the Sea*. Is that correct?"

"Yes, Deputy we do. In fact my daughter and her husband are staying there this week. They should have arrived Monday evening. My youngest daughter, Roamy, is staying with their children, here in Fredericksburg. I've tried to reach them by phone but I haven't been able to get through. I've tried several times and finally I called the phone company and they said the phone line was down or something. I asked them to please check it out. I've been especially worried since we heard about the plague epidemic on the island, and I hadn't heard from them and now the quarantine and all. Is something the matter? Why the inquiry? They're all right, aren't they?"

"Mrs. Reinhold, by any chance is the Judge home?"

"The Judge passed away recently. Why do you ask? Something's the matter and you're not telling me. Am I right?"

"Ma'am, we don't know. There's a Black Lincoln Navigator under your house and a green Plymouth van. Do either of those belong to your daughter and her husband?"

"The black Navigator. They recently leased it. I don't know anything about a green van."

"Ma'am, what is your daughter's married name?"

"Wissenhunt. Her husband's name is JB, that is, that's what we call him. His real name is Jon Barton, Jon with no H. J-O-N."

"Mrs. Reinhold, what does your daughter look like?"

"She's thin, blonde, pretty, blue eyes. Why? Has she been hurt?"

"Ma'am, we've been going house-to-house down here trying to get everyone inoculated against the plague and one of our nurses has disappeared. She disappeared in the vicinity of *Hatteras by the Sea* and yesterday I visited your cottage and spoke to someone who said he was Mister Wissenhunt. I didn't see him because he spoke through the door, but he said that neither he nor his wife were going to open the door until the plague was over. He did say though that they'd both had their shots. Now, no one is answering the door. Ma'am, may we have your permission to force entry if necessary?"

"Do you mean to break into the house?"

"Yes, ma'am, I do."

"Couldn't they be out somewhere? No, you said that they wouldn't leave the cottage. The green van must be someone they know, maybe some friend. I am worried, Deputy, very worried. Yes, go ahead, find out what's going on and please call me right back. I'll be waiting by the phone. I'm going to contact my attorney . . . But you have my permission, Deputy Hale, to do whatever you deem necessary to find my daughter . . . and of course JB. Just go ahead."

"Thank you, Mrs. Reinhold."

Matt and I jumped into the car and I filled him in as we sped down the street to the Reinhold cottage. I didn't feel good about this, no not at all. When we arrived and were told that the phone lines had been cut, I felt even worse.

Lieutenant Howard, tore out the screen on a double hung Anderson triple pane window on the main deck and then broke the window and raised it to gain entry to the house. He then hurried around and opened the front door.

While Matt and I stayed on the deck near the front door, Lieutenant Randy Howard and Jerry Wilson took several deputies and with guns drawn and wearing surgical masks they quickly checked out the entire house. A grim Randy reported back to Matt.

"We've found the nurse. She's all right, but in shock. She heard us come into the bedroom and started pounding on the closet door. She was locked in a closet up stairs. She's had the hell frightened out of her, but she hasn't really been harmed. She's on her way out. We have two bodies, male and a female. Male, probably Mister Wissenhunt, was found in the powder room on this floor, looks to have been shot or stabbed in the chest. Dead awhile. Female, master bedroom, dead on the bed, probably Mrs. Wissenhunt. She's tied to the bed, doesn't seem to be stabbed or shot. Could be strangled. Now, the bizarre. There's a black woman's head wrapped in a towel on a chair in that same bedroom. Haven't found a body as yet. Could it be the girl from Edenton?"

"Probably is. What about Capisano?"

Randy grinned. "I was saving that 'till last,

Boss."

"Really?"

"We got him! On the ten most wanted list, and we got him. He's in the same room we found the nurse in. She identified him. He's on the bed and he's puked all over it and himself and he's coughing up all kinds of crap and blood. He's a mess. Nobody's gone near him. He's just lying there on his stomach with a big knife in his hand breathing real heavy. I ain't touching the sonofabitch. Nurse says he's got the plague. Jerry Wilson and two deputies are holding weapons on him. Matt, we're going to need some . . . gloves? . . . I don't know what we're going to need to handle him. I told them if he moves a muscle to shoot him."

Matt sucked in his cheeks and with his head down looked up at Lieutenant Howard. "Looks like we have a situation, Randy. You should have taken his knife and cuffed him."

"He ain't going anywhere, Sheriff."

"You should have cuffed him."

"Matt, I'm not touching the bastard, and I can't ask someone else to, not without gloves. They could catch that . . ."

"Well, Randy what do you . . ."

Bam! Bam! Bam! Three muffled shots from

inside the house. "What the hell was that?" Matt asked, but Randy was already gone. Matt turned to me. "What the hell, Fred?"

"I don't think we have to worry about Jack Capisano, Matt."

Nurse Sandy Garrett burst through the door with help from a deputy. She was moving slowly and looked scared. She was wearing her lab jacket and her clothes and hair were disheveled, but she didn't appear to have a serious injury. She stood at the deck rail and looked back toward the street and started sobbing. Matt gave the deputy a nod that had only one meaning – get that woman the hell out of here and fast.

And he did.

Randy Howard returned. "Well Matt, we don't have a situation anymore. It seems Mister Capisano rolled to the side of the bed and sat up but wouldn't drop the knife. He stood up and took a step toward the deputies and they carried out their orders. Two slugs in the upper body and one between the eyes. All three fired once."

"Who was the marksman, Randy?"

"I didn't ask."

"Don't."

Chapter 17

At a little past five o'clock Thursday afternoon, Jo Anne and I and Sheriff Matt and Sergeant Mel Norrick of the State Police were sitting on my front deck enjoying my good scotch and musing about the life and times of Jack Capisano.

"You going to have a shooting inquiry, Matt," Norrick asked.

"Already had one. Randy's doing the paper work now. It was a righteous, clean shooting."

"And it brought a nice simple end to what could have been a logistics and bureaucratic nightmare," I added.

"From what I've heard," Jo Anne said, "Jack Capisano seems to have been a disturbed, vagabond, serial killer with a gift for taxidermy and a penchant for collecting women's heads. I just can't believe that in his suitcase you all found eleven tanned faces, skins . . . ah, what are they? Masks? That's eleven lives he destroyed that we know of and he used to sit on this deck and . . ."

I interrupted. "Babe, you're not counting the black girl and Sylvia Wissenhunt and her husband and the Hyatt guy he killed before he fled last year. That's what, fifteen we know about?"

"More than that," Matt said. "How about his mother, or whatever she was, and her boyfriend, and it goes on and on."

"And we forgot Irene Sanderson," Jo Anne added.

"Christ, how could I forget her?" I said. "I guess I blocked that out and I'm trying to not remember."

Mel Norrick twirled his leaded crystal glass around in his big hand slopping the dark Johnnie Walker Black over the ice cubes and said, "So, this sonofabitch killed like twenty people. That's approaching John Wayne Garcey who buried thirty-some boy's bodies under his house. Hell of a way to be remembered. If he hadn't done that, no one would know who in the hell he was. What are you going to do with all those head skins . . . I mean his collection of faces, Matt?"

"I don't know . . . it looks like maybe we have a situation here. I doubt if anyone has ever had to worry about this before. You certainly don't send them back to relatives. As always, I'm open to suggestions . . . and I might add that if I don't hear any good ones, I'm putting Mister Hale here in charge of body parts distribution."

Upon hearing of my possible new tasking, I retreated from the deck and returned shortly with a bucket of ice and a half gallon of dear old Johnnie. No one was going anywhere until Matt had a suitable solution to his latest situation, and you could take that to the bank.

Meanwhile, at the Medical Center, Bill Hedgepath and Tom Allen sat side by side in the lab preparing a series of new tests using the unproven antibiotics sent from CDC that afternoon. They were interrupted by Shawn Caldwell who was in charge of the call-in service that had been set up at the Medical Center to ensure that everyone on the island had been inoculated against the plague. Radio stations, Falcon Cable and sound trucks had all been used in an attempt to contact the people and now call-in was established to answer questions and manage the inoculations of those who had been overlooked or somehow left out.

"Doctor Hedgepath, there's a call for you from a Doctor Gregory at the Centers for Disease Control in Atlanta," Shawn said. "Do you want to take the call in here?"

"Yes, thank you, I will."

"It's the flashing third light, Doctor."

Doctor Allen reached to his right, picked up the phone that was on a long cord and passed it behind his back and to his left to Bill Hedgepath.

"Doctor Hedgepath, here!" He barked. "Crandall, what's the story on the Indian work with antibiotic triflurpenometholoxin? . . . and? . . . and, so where does that leave us? . . . When? . . . We could have a lot of lives hanging in the balance . . . and, okay, that sounds good. Now listen, inform every-one. We need to be covered on this. Doctors Hardy and Allen will make that determination. Thank you, Crandall, keep in touch."

Doctor Hedgepath thought for a minute then passed the telephone back to Tom Allen. "I've got good news and better news," he said.

"Let's hear it."

"The Indians have completed numerous trials with the drug to fight several pulmonary diseases including two cases of pneumonic plague and several cases of second stage meningococcemia. With the plague, one lived and one died. With the mening, I'm sure you're aware second stage is more than 80% fatal and they've had 100% survival rate.

So, there's been limited patient success when given in the proper dose and it's properly prepared with proper attention to detail."

"What's that mean?"

"Well, there have been deaths, but the Indians have developed a decent trial table for age and body weight but it can't be given too late in the infection, and it only works with O negative blood."

"Then it's not worth a damn! It's not good for most people."

"Let me finish. Remember, I told you that the sequence was absorption in aluminum hydroxide, and diluted with saline solution, and then added to a fresh quart of blood, not the patients, and allowed to assimilate there, and then given to the patient through transfusion."

"I remember. Okay, I got it. That quart of blood has to be O negative. O negative is the universal donor, so it can be given to anyone once it's properly mixed. Do they have time studies?"

"Yes."

"When can we get the drug? We can get it, right?"

"Yes, we can get it. A sufficient quantity for 500 doses for adult males will arrive in New York early tomorrow morning. Our jet will fly it down here, to Hatteras. That's all arranged . . ."

"Damn, you guys are life savers. This is coming with tables and instructions, etc.?"

"That should be coming to Bideus this evening through a computer dump." Doctor Hedgepath smiled a broad smile and removed his glasses. "And as far as we being life savers, well, that's what we're in business for isn't it . . . but . . . remember what Bideus said when he quoted old Sherlock Holmes about not counting your chickens before they're hatched. It might work, but this stuff just might not work with this hardy, mean critter we have to kill. So, Doctor Allen, how many quarts of O negative blood do we have to round up and get down here to give this concoction a chance to shine?"

Back in his house, Sheriff Mathews closed the door and bolted it. Living in Hatteras Village, it was an oddly needless precaution, but one he took every night since becoming Sheriff of Dare County. There were a lot of nuts out there. Matt switched on the living room lights, though it wasn't yet dark, went to the kitchen and poured himself a half glass of vodka, added some ice and Perrier from the refrigerator, and returned to the living room, where he settled into his favorite old blue recliner.

Matt was thirsty and he drank half the glass down. It seemed to him that for the past few days he had been unable to quench his thirst and all that water had caused him to constantly have to urinate and urinating burned.

He reached over to his side table and opened a box of small cigars and extracted one and lit it with a match from the box of kitchen matches sitting on the table next to the cigar box. He puffed out several clouds of smoke and suddenly he was dizzy. He felt tired and weak. There was a tingling in his hands and he dropped his glass, spilling it on himself and the chair.

His hands continued to tingle and he wondered if he was having a heart attack. His vision blurred and he felt hot and he reached for the telephone on the side table knocking the base onto the floor as he grabbed the receiver. He was now certain he was having a heart attack and was about to pass out. He felt around on the floor for the telephone base found it and placed it in his wet lap. With great effort he dialed 911 and then all went black as he dropped the phone while falling forward out of the chair and onto the carpet.

Chapter 18

When Sheriff Mathews awoke, he was lying on the examining table in the emergency room of the Hatteras Medical Center. An IV drip tube was suspended near the table and attached to the back of his right hand by a needle taped in place. The first face he saw was of tall, skinny, angular, Doctor Porter Hardy.

"Well, Sheriff, back with us, huh?"

"What happened?"

"You went into a diabetic coma. You're attached to an insulin drip right now."

"I'm not diabetic."

"Well, you are now and it's serious. Your blood sugar level's off the chart. It looks like your pancreas has just about stopped functioning. We don't know what damage you've done to your eyes and kidneys. You should have come to me earlier. If I could get you out of here, I'd send you straight away to Chesapeake General Hospital for at least a week. But I can't, so I'm sending you home where you're to stay in bed and one of the ladies from the Methodist Church will look after you."

"Porter, I can't stay in bed for a week, you know that. And don't pull one of the church volunteers away from the hospice or the Ramada Inn. They're needed there a lot more than they're needed at my bedside. You know I've got family here. Let me call my niece, Dottie, and she'll see after me."

"Matt, you can't call anyone right now. Your blood pressure is very high, and we've got to get your blood sugar down. I don't think you understand your condition. You are lucky to be alive. If you hadn't been able to dial 911 before you passed out, you would probably have died right there on you living room floor."

"I'm sorry, I don't remember. I was at Fred Hale's place and I drove home and fixed myself a drink and that's all I remember."

"You dialed 911 and their equipment disclosed the call was coming from your house. The line was open with no one on it, so they sent a patrol car around and Sergeant Lynch responded and saw your car in the driveway and knocked on the door. When no one responded, he tried the door, found it locked and he looked in the window, where he saw you sprawled on the floor. He broke the door down and called for an ambulance. EMS brought you here. And you have insulin-dependent diabetes which means you may have to take several insulin shots a day for the rest of your life . . . and stay off the booze. Hey, don't look so grim. It's not the end of the world. Look, Matt, with this form of diabetes, the body is forced to obtain energy from body fat instead of glucose and a huge build up of glucose occurs and that often leads to a diabetic coma and unconsciousness. Your pancreas just isn't producing enough insulin to break down the glucose."

"Why does it show up now?"

"Probably, because you're under terrible stress. You're not sleeping right, your blood pressure's up, you just caught a serial killer, you're fighting the plague, as well as worrying about Hurricane Dixie, and not eating right. You're going to the john every couple of hours, and you're always thirsty. Matt, anything that raises your blood pressure or makes you ill increases your need for insulin. This whole thing may have been triggered by your plague shot, who knows? What I do know is if you don't take care of yourself right now you're going to do irreparable damage to yourself. In the next few hours your blood sugar will start dropping and we can breathe a little easier. Matt, I realize that this is a bad time and you need to do a little planning, so I'll let you talk to one deputy right now. Who's it going to be?"

"Call . . . Randy Howard and tell him to get his ass over here."

"He's in the waiting room."

Friday, dawned a beautiful day. Clear skies and no wind, but Hurricane Dixie was headed right for us.

I learned from The Weather Channel that the 0200 position was 31.2 degrees north and 65.7 degrees west traveling at 10 miles per hour with a course of 300 degrees and a wind speed that had picked up to 104 miles per hour. The pressure was 957 millibars and continuing to fall so greater wind speeds could be expected. The Hurricane Center in Miami had now issued a Hurricane Watch for the east coast of the United States from Myrtle Beach, South Carolina to Atlantic City, New Jersey, and were expecting to issue a Hurricane Warning tomorrow morning.

The warning would give us 24 hours notice that

we were about to be hit with winds of at least 74 miles per hour and associated rough seas. On the present track the hurricane would pass about sixty miles south of Bermuda and was now located only about 620 miles from Cape Hatteras.

To add to our apprehension, the forecasters said that they were relatively certain that the winds would greatly increase when the storm reached the Gulf Stream. It seems the barometer pressures and the conditions were similar to those that influenced Hurricane Andrew which was the costliest of record and tore up Florida in 1992. If I remember correctly those winds reached more than 140 miles per hour.

Our "little strip of sand" couldn't survive a category four hurricane and that was what they were talking about with winds of 131-155 miles per hour and storm surge of some 18 feet above normal. If that happened, Hatteras Island would be devastated, and with our quarantine, there would be a dreadful loss of life. I was beginning to wonder just what we Outer Bankers had done to really piss off the gods.

The early morning Norfolk TV news informed me that there were now 81 people diagnosed with the plague on Hatteras Island but that neither the Centers for Disease Control in Atlanta nor the island physicians would confirm the numbers.

A reporter, one Alice Bannerman, reported live from the Bonner Bridge roadblock that she had reliable reports that panic was running rampant throughout Hatteras Island and that the State Police and the Dare Sheriff's Department were greatly under manned and could not control the situation. She also reported that the Coast Guard was having difficulty keeping people on the island and had turned back an armada (fleet) of boats heading for the mainland.

The people of Ocracoke were reported leaving their island in droves and taking the ferries south to Swan Quarter and Cedar Island.

I'd never heard such bullshit. Unless things had changed a lot since I went to bed at around midnight last night, after a brief meeting with Lieutenant Randy Howard, everything was under control and the folks of Hatteras Island were holding up like troopers. It was possible we did have 80 some sick with the plague and more deaths than I knew about, and I wasn't aware of what was going on over on Ocracoke, but I doubted if what had been reported was true, because the rest was pure bullshit. Next, one of us Bankers would hear from the *National Enquirer* or *Late Edition* or *American Journal* or *Hard Copy* or some such TV group offering to pay $20 to buy our "story."

I had to chuckle when the newsman holding down the early morning Anchor Desk profusely thanked reporter "Little Miss Alice Blue Gown" for her update and for showing great calm and fortitude in the face of such horrific conditions and how all in the newsroom hoped to see her return soon safely to Norfolk.

Alice's sign off was indeed dramatic. "Well, thank you, John, and if there's a story here on the Outer Banks, I'll be here. No matter what, you can count on that."

And if a bull frog had wings he wouldn't bump his ass. Please, let's all stand for the National Anthem!

Chapter 19

After breakfast, our last two eggs I might add, I immediately drove to Sheriff Matt's home and knocked on the door. It was opened by a pretty, dark haired, barefoot lass of about 25 dressed in cut off jeans and amply filling a white halter top.

"Is the Sheriff receiving, Dottie?"

"Hi, Fred. He's in the bed but awake and grouchy. He's not allowed to see any television until his blood sugar is back to normal and no radio either, so he just lies there and grumbles. Come on in."

"Are you feeling all right?"

"Oh, I'm fine, but my arm's sore. Your family is okay, I hope."

"Jo Anne is just fine. Also complaining about a

sore arm."

I've been using Uncle Mathews' telephone to call everyone I know and tell them what's going on. Wait until he gets the bill, then he'll have something to grouse about. Would you like some coffee?"

"No, thanks," I mumbled following her through the house and remembering that I'd had her coffee before. There wasn't enough sugar and cream on the island to make it drinkable. Maybe that's why she still wasn't married. In my day a morning cup of coffee was a man's first priority. I suspect now though that has changed a little to Diet Coke or Diet Pepsi with a bowl of trail mix or a cherry pop tart.

Matt was propped up in bed with a stainless steel stand next to the bed holding an IV bag. His dark hair was combed and he had shaved, though he always carries a five o'clock shadow.

"Good Morning, sir."

"Good morning, Fred. What did you do with the faces?"

"Ah, glad you asked. I turned them over to the County Medical Examiner for proper identification."

"And that would be?"

"Porter Hardy for this week."

"And what did he do with them?"

"Put them in the freezer."

"So, you effectively passed the buck."

"Was that a question or a statement?"

"A statement. So, how's everything going from your end?"

"Doctor Allen is working his ass off trying to find an antibody that kills this plague. A hell of a lot of people have come down with it and we can't figure out how they're getting it. It's being passed somehow. One good point though. If you got your shot before exposure it seems to make you immune. But if after, its not much help. I guess the bacteria is just too aggressive. I gotta tell you, Matt, the church women are doing one hell of a good job and none of them has caught it."

"I'm sure they'd appreciate your expressing it that way, Fred. But you're right, this village hangs together in troubled times. Always has . . . where's the hurricane?"

"About 450 miles from here. Presently, a category two but expected to upgrade to a category three in the next 24 hours."

"And the winds are now?"

"104-105. It takes 111 to become a category three."

"Yes, I know . . . What the hell are we gonna do if it hits here in the middle of all this? I can't pull people out of their homes and assemble them in some place like the school. That could be a death warrant."

"I agree with you. Luckily, we have very few locals who live on the ocean front. They either can't afford to or they're too smart to. So, evacuation of the ocean front shouldn't be too difficult."

"Where we gonna put them?"

"Other rental cottages away from the beach and now that I think about it, the sound, too."

"The Park Rangers who live on the island could coordinate that. They could get the word out, set up a center. Who knows every cottage on the island?"

"Only one man, Matt. Dan Johnson, Midgett Realty."

"Good idea. Set it up. Put Dan in charge. I'll have Randy Howard contact the Rangers. I feel better already."

"Good thing you do Uncle Matt, 'cause it's time for another blood sugar test," Dottie said as she came through the bedroom door. "Give me your finger and don't whine little buckaroos."

A little past noon Doctor Tom Allen and Doctor Bill Hedgepath sat on high stools in the Medical Center lab and discussed their plan of attack. Doctor

Allen was saying, "Bill, if we go the regular route, the standard petri dish, stain test, it'll take us 12-24 hours to get conclusive results as to the effectiveness of this stuff."

"Right, what do you want to do?"

"I want you to do that, Bill. Everything by the book. I'm going to go right to the patient. I think I have enough data to do that. It might not work but if it does it will save numerous lives. As attending physician I take the responsibility."

"Wait. I have an idea. Let's do an almost test. We'll take a pint of blood from the patient and mix up our potion and mix it with the patient's blood and try different strengths. If it works like it's supposed to, as a toxic shock, then we'll know."

"We'll know if it works there, and at least we'll know more than we do now. I agree, let's do it."

"Who's your first patient?"

"My first lab rat is Katy Lee, a twenty-one year old woman who will surely die if this doesn't work."

At one thirty testing was ready to begin. The blood from Katy Lee had been drawn and brought to the lab, the Triflurpenometholoxin had been dosed for a body weight of 140 pounds and absorbed in aluminum hydroxide, properly diluted with saline solution, and added to a quart of O negative blood and allowed to assimilate throughout the quart.

"Okay, Bill, how much of this do we use with the pint of Katy Lee's blood?"

"I've got it right here in this beaker. It's based on body weight, the amount of blood in the body and proportioned to this pint."

"You're the note taker, Bill, and keeper of the scientific record, are we ready to commence?"

"Yes."

"Then let's do it . . . God, man, you know, I feel like Doctor Salk when he was testing his vaccine for polio. My heart's beating so loud I can hear it."

"Just remember, he had a lot of misses before he got it right."

Doctor Allen shut his eyes, said a little prayer and mixed the Triflurpenometholoxin solution with Katy Lee's blood.

The two o'clock newscast informed all that Hurricane Dixie was 480 miles from Cape Hatteras with maximum winds that had reached 111 miles per hour and that the storm had been re-classified as a category three hurricane with wind speeds of 111-130 MPH. The storm had picked up speed and was now traveling at 18.5 MPH in a west northwest direction of 288 degrees true, and the barometer had fallen to 955 millibars. Could the hurricane still miss us? Yes, of course it could. Would it? No one was taking any bets. Dare Building Supply had sold out of plywood before noon and now folks were buying any kind of lumber they could to batten down the hatches. So far the skies were clear, the wind about 5 knots from the southwest, but some noticed that the ocean surf had picked up a little and high tide was a bit higher than usual. Jo Anne and I started moving everything that wasn't nailed down from the bottom floor of our house up to the main level some 14 feet above mean high tide.

Before nightfall we'd also move our vehicles to the highest ground on Hatteras Island, the dune area around the airport. In all the storms to hit Hatteras since people have owned autos, one parked at the airport has never taken on water. Hey, that information is good enough for me. Now I had to find a car that made sense to sacrifice, and I had one in mind. A green van with Florida plates parked over at Judge Reinhold's cottage in a subdivision called *Hatteras by the Sea*. The owner wouldn't be needing it any time soon.

Chapter 20

Both Doctors sat with eyes glued to their microscopes. Live plague bacteria were evident in Katy Lee's treated blood. Tom Allen felt like a sniper peering through his scope and waiting for that one moment when he knew a kill was certain. His body tingled and his breathing was shallow.

Bill Hedgepath was wired tight. His stomach was churning as though he had the winning lottery ticket. He was sure of it. All they had to do was call out the six numbers and he'd win. No question about it. So, what was the hold up? Why weren't the little bastards dying? "Tom, don't you think we should have seen something by now? Some reaction?"

"You'd think so, as toxic as this stuff is. I'm

still getting movement. Not what I expected. This stuff should kill them dead. It shouldn't work like your generic antibiotic that stops reproduction and relies on the immune system to follow up. This should kill them dead and fast . . . you know, maybe it's working, but slowly . . . Bill, perhaps we didn't make the solution strong enough. We'll just have to watch a while longer. I'm going to try another slide. You know, it's possible that it won't work in the lab but will in the human body. Maybe there are too many bacteria."

"Everything you say is certainly true, I was talking to Joan Savage earlier this morning . . ."

"What's she been doing? I haven't seen her here in a while."

"She's doing the record and forwarding everything on every patient to CDC. It's a big job, and I know you aren't fond of her, but I believe that once . . ."

"Hey!"

"What do you have?"

"Look in here! This second slide. Check it out."

He replaced Tom Allen at his microscope. "No movement. None!" Bill gleefully shouted.

Tom leaned into Bill's microscope and peered into the eye piece. "There's still movement on your slide. Dead on one, movement on the other. Ideas?"

"Yes. Our mixture hadn't fully assimilated throughout Katy's sample of blood. We had hot spots. The hot spots killed and killed fast, but the toxicity of the hot spot might be so strong as to kill her if it were the same throughout her bloodstream. If we had some way to measure the difference in toxicity between the two blood slides then . . . WE DO! Bideus."

"Bideus?"

"Yes. Bideus. He brought a special scanner that can measure relative degrees of toxemia. He can scan these slides, no, first he has to scan our triflurpenometholoxin mixture. He gets a reading and . . . dammit, I'm not sure how it works, but it can give us a relative toxicity reading between our base mixture and the quantity of triflurpeno that's in the blood on the two slides. I'm certain of that. It's all tied through modems to CDC's computers. I'll get him right on it."

Friday evening, Katy Lee's mother, Bobbie Adams, stood at the door of room 246 in the Ramada Inn wearing a surgical mask and gloves and greeted Doctors Porter Hardy, Tom Allen and Bill Hedgepath also similarly mask protected. As the men stepped through the doorway they saw Katy Lee on her back in a double bed hooked up to an

IV and with an oxygen line in her nostrils. She appeared to be asleep.

Doctor Hardy asked, "What was her latest temperature, Bobbie?"

"Hundred and fi-ve," she said in her muffled South Carolina drawl. "Can't we do something more? I don't know if Katy Lee's asleep or unconscious." Tears filled her eyes and she wiped at them with her finger tips. "I'm sorry, I'm just so distraught."

Tom Allen spoke up. "Bobbie, with your permission, we're going to try something new. As you are aware, we took some blood from Katy Lee earlier and we've been testing it with a new drug and procedure. It's risky and it hasn't been tested extensively in the U.S., but it has undergone some testing in India, and they've had good results with several pulmonary diseases. But I have to tell you that of the pneumonic plague patients that were given this therapy, one died and one lived. That's the extent of the world's experience with this procedure to combat plague.

"Bobbie, I'm leveling with you. In my opinion, and Porter and Doctor Bill Hedgepath both agree with me, unless there's a miracle, Katy Lee is going to die. We've now done everything we can for her and it's up to her immune system to overwhelm the infection. That's not going to happen. It's already a miracle that she's lived as long as she has. Others have not. If she were Catholic, we'd recommend that she be given her last rites."

"Tom, why are you being so cruel to me? Can't you give me some hope?"

"All I can offer is this new procedure."

"Can you tell me what it is?"

"Yes. We have a drug called triflurpenometho- loxin that's a poison. It kills bacteria but we haven't learned all we need to know about giving it to patients. It's a shock treatment. And the trick is to kill an aggressive bacteria that has infected the body without killing the patient. Dosage is dependent on body weight and perhaps individual metabolism. The heaviest person to receive a dose for plague was 40 kilos and that's around 90 pounds. Katy Lee is 140 pounds."

"What you're saying is that the treatment may kill her."

"Yes."

"Have you tried it here on anyone else, yet?"

"No."

"It's my decision?"

"Yes."

"How long before we'd know something?"

"Not long."

"Do it!"

It took an hour to complete the set up in Katy Lee's room and to fashion a makeshift lab in a spare motel room and to ensure that the doctors had sufficient supplies and instruments in case they had what they were calling a medical emergency. Bobbie agreed to wait in the lab, but would be called if anything significant occurred.

After Susan, the attending nurse, completed the EKG hook up and the transfusion IV at twelve past seven, the three doctors hovered over Katy Lee's bed waiting for a reaction.

7:14 She opened her eyes.

7:16 She began coughing up phlegm and blood.

7:19 She began having minor convulsions. Irregular EKG. Blood sample taken.

7:23 She began having major convulsions and had to be restrained. EKG off the chart.

7:25 Doctors consider a tranquilizer but opt against it as her weakened state might cause cardiac arrest. First blood sample shows live bacteria.

7:32 Transfusion completed and IV saline solution started to fight dehydration. Blood sample taken. Convulsions continue.

7:33   Cardiac arrest. Commenced CPR.
7:34   Heart beat. Regular EKG. No convulsions.
7:39   Second sample shows live bacteria.
7:44   Patient remains unconscious. Heart rate steady. Breathing shallow.
7:48 Third blood sample taken. Second saline IV given.
8:05   Reduced bacterial activity.

"What exactly does that mean, Tom?" Porter Hardy asked.

"It means what I said. There is definitely reduced activity. Susan take another blood sample. I want to be certain of what we have."

After Tom Allen left with the blood sample, Porter Hardy and Bill Hedgepath stood quietly for several minutes on either side of Katy Lee's bed, each with his own thoughts. Finally, Porter Hardy said, "What do you think, Bill."

Doctor Bill Hedgepath's eyes teared above his mask and he shook his head. "I think . . ."

"THE BACTERIA'S DEAD!" Doctor Allen yelled as he opened the room's door. "No activity. I want another sample. But I think we did it. Now all we have to do is keep her alive while her body purges itself."

"As I was saying," Bill continued, "I think Doctor Tom Allen has done a super job and accomplished a major medical breakthrough. In fact, I've decided to recommend him for the CDC Meritorious Service Medal."

Tom Allen's smile could be seen through his surgical mask. "Thanks, Bill, I appreciate it, but let's remember a number of folks made this happen. I do think though that we can tell Miss Katy Lee's mother that through all the trials and tribulations, through all the heartaches and tears . . . hell, as Shakespeare said, through all this sound and fury, a small miracle has happened. And I'm as pleased as punch to have been part of it. Gentlemen, let's go save some more lives."

Chapter 21

Saturday, September 22, a day that would surely end in tragedy, started out beautifully with a gentle easterly breeze, a cloudless sky and a noon temperature of 79 degrees.

Three hundred miles at sea, nature had gone berserk with howling winds and towering waves and rain so heavy that it pounded and flattened the wave tops and shattered water spouts and tornadoes as soon as they were spawned.

All Western Atlantic shipping had been vectored around the storm into which no sane man would venture. The Hurricane Hunters, flyers of huge multiengined aircraft that fly into storms and take weather observations, warned of the worst storm to threaten the east coast of the United States since

Hurricane Andrew in '92.

On a personal note, I was wary but not terrified. Logic told me to get the hell out of here. The government told me I couldn't, and so several thousand of us were on a run-a-way train that sooner or later would reach the end of track. I rationalized that the government was doing what was best for the population as a whole, but it's still hard to accept when you learn you are expendable, a discard, a reject, a threat. But we were, and it would have been inexcusable incompetence, even madness, to allow us to expose the outside to this deadly plague bacteria.

So, thank you very much Mister David Kerry, Counselor at Law, you SONOFABITCH. If you had not selfishly held yourself above the law, you would still have your son, Tom, and Tom would still have his two friends, and another sixteen women, ten men and two children, who had never heard of you or suspected that they had any reason to fear you, would be alive today. Not to mention untold hundreds who wouldn't be sick and scared, and several thousand more who wouldn't be on this barrier island on this day waiting like hogs to the slaughter for a deadly hurricane to steal their treasure and scar their souls.

Our transportation was the now infamous green "murderer's" van, and we were happy to have it and used it to bus folks back from leaving their vehicles at the airport.

The morning weather update had carried the expected Hurricane Warning as well as the prediction that the storm would slam ashore somewhere between Emerald Isle and Nags Head, North Carolina. The present track would make landfall on our neighbor Ocracoke Island. That also meant that in all likelihood Hatteras Village would be in the eye of the tiger. Not good news.

Dixie's 2:00 AM position was 324 miles from Hatteras on a course of west northwest, traveling at 11 miles an hour with sustained winds of 121 miles per hour and gusts to 150. It was still a category three storm but it was building. When the storm crossed the warm Gulf Stream the "hurricane experts" were all forecasting that it would absorb enough energy to become a category four hurricane (winds 131-155 MPH). That forecast wasn't bad news, it was devastating news.

Ocracoke Island had been evacuated. North of Bonner Bridge, the villages of South Nags Head, Nags Head, Kill Devil Hills and Kitty Hawk were all evacuated. People had left Manteo and Manns Harbor, and headed inland for safety. But not us.

The folks on Hatteras Island were quarantined. Some thought it was a death sentence, but I was more hopeful than that.

We were the talk of the air waves. Good Morning America broke the news nationwide at 8:00 and by 8:15 all phone lines to and from the island were jammed. The "hard" news was that we were being sacrificed to contain the plague epidemic that had already taken scores of lives. According to the news sources, our families and friends were calling the Governor and other politicians to plead our case. But it seems everyone was passing the buck to CDC. No one wanted to be blamed for another plague epidemic.

CDC released a statement at 12:45 that said in effect that the plague epidemic was under control, but it was unsafe for people in the Quarantine Area to leave until Sunday evening at the earliest. That was not much help for we were due to be hit between midnight and 1:00 AM Sunday morning. depending of course on several variables.

By noon, Jo Anne and I had completed moving our belongings and other "stuff" from the garage, my work shop, the gym and the guest quarters, to the main floor which was some 14 feet above mean high tide. A category three storm carried with it a surge of 9-12 feet. Not much room for error. We didn't want to think about what would happen if Dixie went to a category four. That carried a 13-18 foot surge and that would be the end of that.

Our great room, the library and my den looked as though we were moving in what with furniture and boxes and electrical tools and junk piled everywhere. Amos was getting nervous.

The most difficult object to move had been the generator. It was heav--y. But considerable lifting and pushing and tugging and swearing brought it up the stairs and onto the main deck where it was then dragged through the sliding glass doors and into the great room where it took its place along side our other valuables like our huge "mobile" propane grill. Believe me, a 5000 kw generator full of fuel needs an elevator. But it was now as safe as I was and I was sure that we'd be needing it and its neighbor if we were still around after Miss Dixie had her way with us.

Trips to the Red and White grocery and Nedo's Shopping Center brought home more candles, flashlight batteries, plastic drop cloths, bottled water and ice.

Folks seem to always forget ice. Very important if you're going to ride out a hurricane of your own volition. Doubly important you're forced to stay, for who knows how much additional booze it will take to put you into total denial and assure you that at the last minute the storm will veer north and leave Hatteras safe and sound.

The wind began to build from the east about 3:30 PM and with the increase in force came the first rain clouds. By the time it started raining, near 4:00, we had filled our bathtubs, shut off the county water, shuttered all our windows, plywooded our doors, and the garage door was down and locked, the outdoor hot tub had been filled to overflowing, the furniture in every room had been covered with plastic drop cloths, and last but not least, we had decided to make our master bedroom our "Fort Apache." Thus, our survival supplies were so located, piled on the carpet in heaps here and there. These special supplies included a battery operated weather radio, TV (satellite and cable), one telephone, one cellular phone, one gallon of Johnnie Walker Black, sufficient ice chests, raincoats and boots, roast beef sandwiches, Twinkies, candy bars, Hershey Kisses, bottled water, and a well equipped first aid kit, numerous flashlights and battle lanterns, and dog supplies.

Needless to say, Amos was worried. He had never been through a hurricane so he didn't know what was going on. Throughout the day he never left my side, no matter where I went or what I did. He was thoughtful but impatient while trying to find something in our actions that was both familiar and reassuring to him. He didn't know he was about to be tested, and if all went well tonight, tomorrow he would be a veteran. He will have survived Hurricane Dixie.

Chapter 22

The full force of the hurricane struck the house a few minutes past midnight.

The sensation was terrifying. I wanted to pull a blanket over my head and disappear, but I could not. My machismo wouldn't allow it.

This wasn't a storm. This wasn't a hurricane. This was violence! It was raw primitive violence.

Like most nasty situations, it had started pleasant enough with a gentle breeze, a light rain, a mist over the sound. Then, like the virgins scattering rose petals in the path of a reigning tyrant, the prelude disappeared and stark reality emerged.

Light winds had changed to blustering winds and then to strong winds and then wild winds and cruel winds. For two hours the house trembled, then shook and was battered and slammed. There was creaking and then crashing and other noises associated with major destruction. Suddenly, we heard a freight train passing close by and then a machine gun stuck on full automatic and then an explosion.

We, three, were huddled together sitting on the bedroom floor. The room was partially lit with two large candles and shadows played games running to and fro across the walls. I was reminded of the first time I went into a Fun House or was it a Tunnel of Love? You bought a ticket and got on the little train and waited with great expectations as the train slowly carried you and your friends into the scary unknown. Afterward we stood around and beat our breasts and lied about how brave we had been, and we bought another ticket. But not right away.

The explosion made the house rock and Jo Anne screamed and Amos growled and began forcefully licking my face. I asked myself – What the hell was that? — but I had no answer. A propane tank? A house exploding? In my mind's eye I saw shingles flying from the roof, windows broken and decks and stairs washed away. People were screaming and drowning and floating and sinking under the . . . surge. The surge, a wall of water erasing our attempt to bring modern civilization to the barrier islands. Had it been a joust with futility? Was this nature's attempt to reclaim its rightful property? Suddenly, I was certain that the bedroom floor was moving or was it the whole house. Were we afloat? Was the carpet wet? Had the house been ripped from its pilings? And then I remembered a slogan from some TV commercial. "A mind is a terrible thing to waste." Wake up!

The wind stopped.

I could hear nothing. I listened, holding my breath. I heard my companions breathing. I checked my watch. It was five minutes past two. I took a deep breath and slowly let it out. I felt drained.

Jo Anne looked up at me and smiled. "Its over. Did you put the time in your journal?"

I knew it wasn't over, but I said, "All we know for sure is that it's stopped – for now."

"Oh, God," she said, "don't tell me we're in the eye."

We had settled in the bedroom at ten o'clock when the winds were reported to be about 60 miles per hour. The TV was on, we had eaten a good dinner at eight o'clock, we were apprehensive but controlled. Ten minutes later we lost power. I suspected it had been cut by the power company for it's their policy to stop electrical service when the island winds reach 70 miles per hour. For more than four hours we had been marooned in the bedroom. It was now time to check things out.

I went to the one window I couldn't shutter and flashed the light outside. It was Jo Anne's shelved garden window and it was intact. It wasn't raining, but I still couldn't see much. Just a lot of water everywhere. I hurried to the kitchen and swept the light over the great room. We had covered everything with plastic drop cloths and they were all wet. I swept the light around but couldn't find the source right away. Then, I saw the problem. Near the front east corner, part of the roof was missing. But the big east side window was still covered with plywood and intact.

Jo Anne hollered. "Fred, come look at this!"

She was standing in the kitchen at the door leading to the floor below. She had her flashlight pointing down the steps into the blackness. What I saw scared the hell out of me. WATER. Water was within a couple of feet of the door. I had 6-7 feet of water in my lower floors. And it was still rising. That meant that the water around the house and in the garage had to be 8 or 9 feet deep. Any wave action was on top of that. Waves could soon be beating at my windows. Why was the house still here? It had to be because it hadn't taken much pounding. The water must have risen fast. Would the house now be lifted off the piles? Not my house! I had enough steel holding the house to the piles to build a goddamn gun boat. Hell, maybe two.

I heard static and noticed that Jo Anne had our weather radio in her hand. We had lost the broadcast around 11:30 and it was still lost. I took the radio from her and turned it off. What to do?

We sat in the kitchen, watched the water rise, and waited anxiously for Dixie's eye to move on by. In an hour and a half the water reached the top step and stopped. We smiled and did a high five just as the winds slammed into the west wall of the great room uncovering and shattering the triple picture window. We ran for the bedroom and slammed the door shut.

For the next hour and twenty minutes we huddled in fear as Mother Nature played a rerun of her last visit. Only this time we were on the west side of the house and got the uncut version.

At 6:30 AM we still had no power, no radio and no telephone. Jo Anne had tried the cellular about five AM but to no avail. However, the winds had fallen off and it was becoming light outside, so I felt that we could safely leave the bedroom. We did and we walked into devastation.

I checked the water in the lower floor and it appeared to be about three feet deep. Too deep to wander around in. I unlocked the front door on the east side of the house and took the panels out of the storm door and prized the plywood off. It took awhile, but eventually I was able to see out and was gladdened that I still had a deck. Then my heart sank. The house seemed to be in a lake and my neighbor's cottage (he and wife were in Richmond) was gone. Nothing on the lot. No piles, no nothing. Just three feet of water. A vacant lot. Before I had time to really take everything in, I heard the phone ring. I went back inside and Jo Anne came running and handed it to me.

"It's Sheriff Mathews, Fred," she said.

"Matt! How bad is it?"

"It's bad, real bad, and I'm afraid we're all stuck here for a *time* . . ."

"What's that mean?"

"Means the Village is an island. We have a new inlet that looks to be at least a half mile wide stretching from the Frisco Pier to the old Vet's bait shop. It means in the Village we took at least ten feet of water over Highway 12. There's destruction everywhere and I'm just hopeful that we haven't lost anybody."

"Me, too."

"On a sad note, the storm accomplished something that has eluded the politicians, the environmentalists, the Army Corps of Engineers, and a bunch of concerned citizens."

"And that is?"

"Well, they all screwed around long enough that the question no longer is will we move the lighthouse. The question now is will we replace it?"

"Aw, shit!"

Epilogue

Mother Nature tried to throw us off her barrier island and failed, but her spawn, Hurricane Dixie, will long be remembered as the most savage storm to ever strike the Carolinas. Sustained winds topped 160 MPH and gusts of 195 were recorded in Buxton, a mere ten miles from Hatteras Village. After landfall, Dixie swung north, picked up speed and smashed through Richmond, Annapolis, Philadelphia, and then turned northeast to batter the coast all the way to Augusta, Maine. There it finally swept out to sea and for a last hurrah capsized a Panama chartered "tramp steamer." Damage along Dixie's track is in the billions, the unofficial death toll is 148, the misery index is off the chart, and the Fed's have approved 238 separate disaster relief areas.

Surprisingly, Dixie took no lives on Hatteras Island, but 92% of our structures were damaged and 29% were totally destroyed. In our village 26 rental cottages disappeared and they all had one thing in common. They were all built on 6x6 piles instead of the now standard 8x8's. Steep roofs survived and flatter ones did not. Sound side was hammered worse than oceanfront, but one luxury cottage at *Hatteras by the Sea* did mysteriously explode and its remnants reminds one of a WWII bombing raid.

It's been reported that twin tornadoes flattened Ocracoke Village, but Nags Head was the epicenter of disaster. Five miles of the old highway that skirted the shore is gone and 51 hurricane party thrill seekers lost their lives when an oceanfront condominium complex tumbled into the sea.

According to recent news reports, Cynthia Hale, a Federal Prosecutor, is after Mister David Kerry, Esquire, smuggler. Using terrorist legislation, it seems she may indict him for involuntary manslaughter because his actions contributed directly to the plague deaths. Our final count was 28 dead which kept our total under the 1929 U.S.A. record of 31 in Los Angeles. So thankfully, we don't go into the record books.

The collapse of the lighthouse caused slanderous outbursts and unrestrained finger pointing with all parties refusing to acknowledge any responsibility for the years of fiddling and foot dragging that condemned the magnificent structure. But there is light. President Clinton has requested monies to rebuild Hatteras Light on a protected site with a replica that would incorporate pieces from the original.

So, folks, there is some joy in Mudville and the new lighthouse has become the symbol of our renewed vitality. Even the short ferry ride between Hatteras Village and Frisco has become routine, and property values in Brigand's Bay are shooting up what with Frisco Inlet available for easy fishing access to the Atlantic Ocean.

As could be expected, the T-shirt industry is flourishing, but "I survived Hurricane Dixie" isn't the hot item. That distinction is held by a northeast import with the macho statement that says it all. "Hey, Mother Nature! You want a piece of me?"

Photograph courtesy of Katherine Cook

FRED HALE is a retired naval officer who lives with his wife Jo Anne and his faithful companion Amos in Hatteras Village on North Carolina's Outer Banks. He is the author of *A Sound Affair*, *The Sound of Death*, and *Sound Affects*. He is currently at work on his fifth novel.